TABLE O

CHAPTER		PAGE #
SECTION 1: THE HOLY SPIRIT		
1	THE HOLY SPIRIT IS A PERSON	7
2	THE HOLY SPIRIT CREATED YOU	11
3	THE HOLY SPIRIT IS THE AUTHOR OF THE WORD OF GOD	17
4	THE HOLY SPIRIT IS YOUR ONLY SOURCE OF TRUE JOY, PEACE AND LOVE	21
5	THE HOLY SPIRIT IS GRIEVED BY WRONG CONVERSATION AND CONDUCT	33
6	THE HOLY SPIRIT INTERCEDES FOR YOU CONTINUOUSLY	41
7	THE HOLY SPIRIT LOVES SINGING	47
8	THE HOLY SPIRIT CAN PROVIDE YOU WITH A PRAYER LANGUAGE THAT NOBODY UNDERSTANDS BUT GOD	53
9	THE HOLY SPIRIT IS THE SOURCE OF THE ANOINTING FOR YOUR LIFE	61
10	THE HOLY SPIRIT LOVES TO TALK TO YOU ABOUT EVERYTHING	67

SECTION 2: THE ASSIGNMENT

11 EVERYTHING GOD CREATED WAS CREATED   79
   TO SOLVE A PROBLEM

12 YOU ARE A REWARD TO SOMEONE   83

13 WHAT YOU LOVE MOST IS A CLUE TO YOUR   93
   ASSIGNMENT

14 WHAT YOU HATE IS A CLUE TO SOMETHING   97
   YOU ARE ASSIGNED TO CORRECT

15 WHAT GRIEVES YOU IS A CLUE TO SOMETHING 103
   YOU ARE ASSIGNED TO HEAL

16 YOUR ASSIGNMENT IS GEOGRAPHICAL   107

17 YOUR ASSIGNMENT WILL REQUIRE SEASONS   111
   OF PREPARATION

18 YOUR ASSIGNMENT MAY BE MISUNDERSTOOD 117
   BY THOSE CLOSEST TO YOU

19 YOUR ASSIGNMENT WILL ALWAYS HAVE AN   123
   ENEMY

20 YOU WILL ONLY SUCCEED WHEN YOUR   135
   ASSIGNMENT BECOMES AN OBSESSION

SECTION 3: THE SEED

21 INVENTORY THE SEEDS YOU ALREADY   141
   POSSESS

22 LEARN THE SECRET OF GIVING YOUR SEED   149
   A SPECIFIC ASSIGNMENT

23 WAIT LONG ENOUGH FOR YOUR SEED TO   153
   PRODUCE YOUR DESIRED HARVEST

24 BE WILLING TO BEGIN YOUR HARVEST WITH   161
    A SMALL SEED

25 QUALIFY THE SOIL   165

26 SOW CONSISTENTLY   171

27 SOW PROPORTIONATE TO THE HARVEST YOU   179
    DESIRE

28 NEVER REBEL AGAINST AN INSTRUCTION FROM 185
    A FINANCIAL DELIVERER GOD HAS ANOINTED
    TO UNLOCK YOUR FAITH

29 ALWAYS SOW WITH THE EXPECTATION OF   197
    A RETURN

30 SOW INSTANTLY IN OBEDIENCE TO THE   221
    HOLY SPIRIT WITHOUT REBELLION OR
    NEGOTIATION

31 THE GREATEST SUCCESS SECRET GOD HAS   229
    EVER TAUGHT ME

Unless otherwise indicated, all Scripture quotations are taken from the King James Version of the Bible.
The 3 Most Important Things In Your Life
ISBN 1-56394-078-7/B-101
Copyright © 2001 by **MIKE MURDOCK**
All publishing rights belong exclusively to Wisdom International
Publisher/Editor: Deborah Murdock Johnson
Published by The Wisdom Center · 4051 Denton Hwy. · Ft. Worth, Texas 76117
1-817-759-BOOK · 1817-759-2665 · 1-817-759-0300
MikeMurdockBooks.com

≈ Acts 2:2 ≈

"And suddenly there came a sound from Heaven as of a rushing mighty wind, and it filled all the house where they were sitting."

Section 1

THE HOLY SPIRIT

❧ John 14:16 ❧

"And I will pray the Father, and He shall give
you another Comforter, that He may abide
with you for ever."

❧ **1** ❧

THE HOLY SPIRIT IS A PERSON

He Is Not Wind, Fire or A White Dove.

Jesus knew this. He taught us, "And I will pray the Father, and He shall give you another Comforter, that He may abide with you for ever," (John 14:16).

He is not an "it."

He is..."Him."

You see, the pictures, metaphors and emblems used in the Bible can easily be misinterpreted and distorted.

The Holy Spirit is a Person, not merely a presence. He is a Person who *has* a presence, an atmosphere emanating from Him. I think the word "spirit" confuses many.

"Oh, she has such a wonderful *spirit* about her!" said a minister's wife to me. She was referring to the *attitude* of another lady.

"Oh, I love the *spirit* in this church!" This kind of statement refers to the atmosphere and climate existing in a building.

But, The Holy Spirit is not an attitude, atmosphere or environment. He is a Person who talks, thinks, plans and is incredibly brilliant and articulate. He is the *voice* of the Godhead to us. Read John 16:13, "...He shall not speak of Himself; but whatsoever He shall hear, that shall He speak." A presence or an atmosphere does not talk! A *person* speaks.

A presence or an atmosphere does not have a will, a mind or a *plan*. Thoughts have presence. Birds generate a presence.

The Holy Spirit is much more than a presence. You see, aroma is not really the food. The stink is not the skunk! The bark is not the dog. The quack is not the duck.

His presence is *evidence* of His Person.

Few people know this. That is why they never discuss their problems with Him. Most believe that He is a silent cloud or wind receiving Assignments to different buildings or people.

Jesus recognized Him as a Mentor. "He shall teach you all things," (John 14:26).

He is not merely a fog.

He is not merely a wind.

He is not merely fire.

He is not merely rain.

He is not merely a white dove at a baptismal service. If He were wind, He could not mentor men. If He were a white bird, He could not teach you all the sayings of Jesus. (See John 14:26.) If He were merely fire, He could not impart counsel. The Holy Spirit simply uses various pictures of Himself to reveal His workings, His nature and various qualities about Him.

The Holy Spirit can enter your life like water — refreshing you. "For I will pour water upon him that is thirsty, and floods upon the dry ground: I will pour My Spirit upon thy seed, and My blessing upon thine offspring: And they shall spring up as among the grass, as willows by the water courses," (Isaiah 44:3-4).

The Holy Spirit can enter your life like fire—

purifying you. "And there appeared unto them cloven tongues like as of fire, and it sat upon each of them. And they were all filled with the Holy Ghost, and began to speak with other tongues, as the Spirit gave them utterance," (Acts 2:3-4).

The Holy Spirit can move suddenly and quickly in your life—like wind. "And suddenly there came a sound from Heaven as of a rushing mighty wind, and it filled all the house where they were sitting," (Acts 2:2).

The Holy Spirit will come to you the way that you need Him the most. He can come as a gentle *Nurturer*—like a mother nourishing her starving and dependent child. He can come as a brilliant and articulate *Advisor*—when you are facing a difficult decision. He can come as a comforting *Healer*—when you have been scarred and tormented from a battle.

The Holy Spirit is a Person. When you embrace this truth, your Christian experience will change dramatically, instantly and satisfy every part of your heart and life.

Our Prayer Together...

"Father, teach me to walk and live with my Mentor, my Companion, The Holy Spirit. You are not a fire, wind or rain...You are the Holy One Who created me. In Jesus' name. Amen."

RECOMMENDED INVESTMENTS:
The Holy Spirit Handbook, Volume 1 (Book/B-100/153 pgs)
The Greatest Day of My Life (Book/B-116/32 pgs)
The School of The Holy Spirit, The Greatest Secret of The Universe (Series 1) (CD/CDS-50)

≈ Job 33:4 ≈

"The Spirit of God hath made me, and the
breath of the Almighty hath given me life."

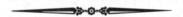

❧ 2 ❧

THE HOLY SPIRIT CREATED YOU

You Are His Greatest Product.

Job knew this. "The Spirit of God hath made me, and the breath of the Almighty hath given me life," (Job 33:4).

Your personality, body and everything about you are the designs of The Holy Spirit. Think of this incredible body that functions miraculously. "I will praise Thee; for I am fearfully and wonderfully made: marvellous are Thy works; and that my soul knoweth right well," (Psalm 139:14).

Your body is His temple. "What? know ye not that your body is the temple of the Holy Ghost which is in you, which ye have of God, and ye are not your own?" (1 Corinthians 6:19).

The Holy Spirit was involved in the creative designing of the temple through Solomon. "And the pattern of all that he had by the spirit, of the courts of the house of the Lord, and of all the chambers round about, of the treasuries of the house of God, and of the treasuries of the dedicated things," (1 Chronicles 28:12).

The Holy Spirit was involved in the creation of the earth at the beginning. "And the earth was without form, and void; and darkness was upon the face of the deep. And the Spirit of God moved upon the face of the waters," (Genesis 1:2).

The Holy Spirit is the One sent to form new

creations on earth. "Thou sendest forth Thy Spirit, they are created: and Thou renewest the face of the earth," (Psalm 104:30).

The Holy Spirit appears to be the One who decides the very shape of every animal. "By His spirit He hath garnished the Heavens; His hand hath formed the crooked serpent," (Job 26:13).

The Holy Spirit is the spirit of life within you that keeps you living and breathing every single moment. "The Spirit of God hath made me, and the breath of the Almighty hath given me life," (Job 33:4). "Thus saith the Lord God unto these bones; Behold, I will cause breath to enter into you, and ye shall live: And I will lay sinews upon you, and will bring up flesh upon you, and cover you with skin, and put breath in you, and ye shall live; and ye shall know that I am the Lord...And shall put My Spirit in you, and ye shall live, and I shall place you in your own land: then shall ye know that I the Lord have spoken it, and performed it, saith the Lord," (Ezekiel 37:5-6, 14).

The Holy Spirit is also the One that gives you the new life after your second birth, the regeneration. "Not by works of righteousness which we have done, but according to His mercy He saved us, by the washing of regeneration, and renewing of the Holy Ghost," (Titus 3:5).

The Holy Spirit is the Source of your life...every part of your life.

The Holy Spirit Is The Giver of Life

Life is a priceless, precious gift to us.
The Giver is The Holy Spirit. "...but the Spirit giveth life," (2 Corinthians 3:6).

The Holy Spirit impregnated Mary, the mother of Jesus. "Now the birth of Jesus Christ was on this wise: When as His mother Mary was espoused to Joseph, before they came together, she was found with child of the Holy Ghost...But while he thought on these things, behold, the angel of the Lord appeared unto him in a dream, saying, Joseph, thou son of David, fear not to take unto thee Mary thy wife: for that which is conceived in her is of the Holy Ghost," (Matthew 1:18, 20).

Think about this incredible truth. The Holy Spirit is the One who ushered in the entry of Jesus, the Son of God, into the earth.

Any words spoken by The Holy Spirit will bring life and energy into you. "It is the spirit that quickeneth; the flesh profiteth nothing: the words that I speak unto you, they are spirit, and they are life," (John 6:63).

The Holy Spirit is the life of God dwelling within you. "Even the Spirit of truth; whom the world cannot receive, because it seeth Him not, neither knoweth Him: but ye know Him; for He dwelleth with you, and shall be in you," (John 14:17).

The Spirit of life is one of the titles of The Holy Spirit. "For the law of the Spirit of life in Christ Jesus hath made me free from the law of sin and death," (Romans 8:2).

The Holy Spirit will breathe life into every person who died in Christ, at the coming of Christ. "But if the Spirit of Him that raised up Jesus from the dead dwell in you, He that raised up Christ from the dead shall also quicken your mortal bodies by His Spirit that dwelleth in you," (Romans 8:11).

The Holy Spirit considers your body His dwelling

place. "Know ye not that ye are the temple of God, and that the Spirit of God dwelleth in you?" (1 Corinthians 3:16).

The Holy Spirit is the Enabler that helps you to keep and protect any good thing God has given you. "That good thing which was committed unto thee keep by the Holy Ghost which dwelleth in us," (2 Timothy 1:14).

The Holy Spirit provides tenacity, strength and determination for those who become dependent and addicted to His presence.

While I was dictating these very words today, something glorious and precious happened. One of my associates walked into the Wisdom Room here, as I was dictating this chapter, with good news. One of my mother sheep had just given birth to a beautiful little black sheep...with a white star on its forehead. I had to stop my dictation, rush out to the yard where all the animals were gathered around the little baby sheep. It was precious. Surrounding the mother and the little baby were many other animals that I have here at my home—several llamas were crowding in trying to nose the little one. Eleazar, my huge camel, wanted to have a part, and Smokey, my miniature donkey, was trying to get his nose in the huddle as well. My antelope were watching from a distance...but it seemed that the entire yard of animals was feeling the glory of life itself—*life! You feel it in the air!*

I thought this was wonderful. While I was writing you about the Giver of all life, right here a few feet from me outside, something He created...a *first*...was just born.

Think for a moment. Look around you at the

incredible animals—antelope, llamas, sheep, goats, camels and behold the incredible imagination of The Holy Spirit in the many ways *He sees methods to generate life and create life!*

I look into trees, and I see beautiful white and blue-green peacocks here at my home. *The Holy Spirit thought of these.*

He created them.

As I look into my aquarium, I see beautiful multi-colored fish swimming smoothly through the water. They were created for the water. He thought of this! How glorious!

The Holy Spirit is the Giver of all life.

The trees are beautiful today. New plants are springing forth. Flowers are beginning to bloom. The Holy Spirit has thought of a million ways to bring life into this earth.

You were His idea.

You are *not* alone.

You have a *destiny*.

You are on His mind all the time.

You are the focus of everything The Holy Spirit will do today.

"What and if ye shall see the Son of man ascend up where he was before? It is the spirit that quickeneth; the flesh profiteth nothing: the words that I speak unto you, they are spirit, and they are life," (John 6:62-63).

Our Prayer Together...
"Precious Holy Spirit, thank You from the depths of my heart for bringing me into Your world. I want to be here. I love being here. I love tasting what You have created. I love beholding,

observing and gazing upon the beauty that You have imagined and brought into being. Thank You for the beautiful animals, the trees and the birds around me. Thank You for my new little black sheep born just seconds ago. Thank You from the depths of my heart for letting me enjoy Your world. Show me how to pleasure You in return. You made me for greatness. You made me to bring pleasure to You. Draw me toward You, Holy Spirit. Draw me toward You today. In the name of Jesus. Amen."

❧ 3 ❧

THE HOLY SPIRIT IS THE AUTHOR OF THE WORD OF GOD

⋙◦⋘

Your Bible Is His Gift To You.

The Holy Spirit breathed through men, the holy Scriptures. "For the prophecy came not in old time by the will of man: but holy men of God spake as they were moved by the Holy Ghost," (2 Peter 1:21).

When you quote the Bible, you are quoting The Holy Spirit. He is articulate, brilliant and authored The Words of God to us today.

He inspired holy men of God to write under the leadership of The Holy Spirit. "All scripture is given by inspiration of God, and is profitable for doctrine, for reproof, for correction, for instruction in righteousness: That the man of God may be perfect, throughly furnished unto all good works," (2 Timothy 3:16-17).

Oh, think of this glorious and incredible Bible we carry around every day! The Holy Spirit spoke every word through 40 people sensitive to Him, over a 1600 year period of time.

▶ He wanted to breathe His *life* into you.

▶ He wanted His *energy* to be poured through you.

▶ He wanted His *Wisdom* deposited in your heart.

▶ He wanted His *instincts* and nature to be

evident and obvious in you.

▶ He wanted you *to know what He knows.*

▶ He wanted you to *feel what He feels.*

▶ He wanted you to *see* what He is looking at.

The Holy Spirit gave you The Word of God as your special weapon, the Sword of the Spirit. "And take the helmet of salvation, and the sword of the Spirit, which is the word of God," (Ephesians 6:17). It is the weapon of The Holy Spirit—the weapon He uses against satan. His *Words* are His destructive weapons that destroy the things of satan.

Jesus used the weapon of The Word, the Sword of the Spirit. When satan tempted Him, Jesus simply answered with the words of The Holy Spirit! "And Jesus answered him, saying, It is written, That man shall not live by bread alone, but by every word of God," (Luke 4:4).

The Holy Spirit led Him into the place where He would be tempted. Then, gave Him the weaponry, (The Word of God) to use against satan. Satan was defeated and angels came to minister to Christ.

So, The Holy Spirit anticipated your warfare. He understands battle. It matters to Him. Your winning is on His mind all the time. He truly has not left you comfortless. He has put His weapon in your *hand*, in your *mouth*, in your *life*.

Treasure His words today. The Word of God is the weapon satan cannot withstand.

Your Bible contains 66 books. These 66 books contain 1189 chapters. Someone estimated that you could read through the entire Bible in 56 hours.

5 Helpful Hints On Reading Your Bible

1.   Establish A Daily Habit. When you read 3 chapters a day (and 5 on Sunday), you will read the entire Bible through within 12 months. When you read 9 chapters each day in the New Testament, you will finish the New Testament every 30 days. When you read 40 chapters a day, you will read the entire Bible every 30 days of your life!

2.   Read At The Same Place Every Day. That should be your Secret Place, where you talk to The Holy Spirit. It should be a private and confidential place away from the traffic of everyone else. Places matter. *Where You Are Determines What Grows In You.*

3.   Read It At The Same Time Each Day. Habit is so powerful. Habits are more powerful than desires. Habit is a gift from God. It simply means that anything you do twice becomes easier. Stop thinking of the word "habit" as a bad word. It is a great word! It is God's easiest way to help you succeed.

4.   Become A Passionate Expert On One Topic In The Bible. Focus and become knowledgeable about that center of your expertise. For example, if you want to study faith, circle every Scripture relating to faith in your personal Bible. Then, create a personal 365 Scripture calendar on the subject of faith. (If you decide to focus on becoming an expert in Scripture on The Holy Spirit—find 365 Scriptures that help you understand The Holy Spirit. Make that your legacy for your family, and teach them a Scripture a day in memorization time.)

5.   Talk Scriptures In Every Conversation. You may be on the phone or in a business transaction—

use the words of The Holy Spirit to answer someone. The Bible becomes your database for your personal opinion.

The Word of God is a tool in the hand of The Holy Spirit to nurture you and furnish you everything you need to succeed on earth. "All scripture is given by inspiration of God, and is profitable for doctrine, for reproof, for correction, for instruction in righteousness: That the man of God may be perfect, throughly furnished unto all good works," (2 Timothy 3:16-17).

As you develop a consciousness of the opinion of The Holy Spirit (the Bible), your whole world will change.

RECOMMENDED INVESTMENTS:
1 Minute Pocket Bible for Fathers (Book/B-51/130 pgs)
1 Minute Pocket Bible for Mothers (Book/B-52/132 pgs)
The Greatest Success Habit on Earth (Book/B-80/32 pgs)

⤳ 4 ⤳

THE HOLY SPIRIT IS YOUR ONLY SOURCE OF TRUE JOY, PEACE AND LOVE

The Holy Spirit Is The Source of Joy.
True success is the presence of joy.

His presence brings joy. "...in Thy presence is fulness of joy; at Thy right hand there are pleasures for evermore," (Psalm 16:11).

His fruit is joy. "But the fruit of the Spirit is love, JOY, peace, longsuffering, gentleness, goodness, faith, Meekness, temperance: against such there is no law," (Galatians 5:22-23).

His Wisdom increases your joy. "Happy is the man that findeth Wisdom, and the man that getteth understanding," (Proverbs 3:13).

The Holy Spirit is the Spirit of Wisdom! "And the Spirit of the Lord shall rest upon him, the Spirit of Wisdom and understanding, the Spirit of counsel and might, the Spirit of knowledge and of the fear of the Lord," (Isaiah 11:2).

True joy is much more than enthusiasm and energy. Many times you may experience the completion of a great project or task and experience enthusiasm. Unfortunately, it normally lasts just a few minutes then your focus changes to another problem to conquer. So your enthusiasm and so-called "joy" are often based on the circumstances of your life and your achievements. Nothing is sadder than to watch someone build their whole life around human achievement in pursuit of joy.

Some pursue money thinking it will produce joy. Yet, the richest people on earth often seem to be the most sorrowful in many circumstances. The famous have been known to commit suicide, even though millions were in their bank accounts.

Some depend on their loved ones to create an atmosphere of happiness. The husband blames the wife for his unhappiness. The wife sometimes blames her husband for her unhappiness. The children blame the parents and their strict rules for their personal loss of joy and enthusiasm. The unemployed blame the economy for their lack of joy.

5 Wrong Conceptions People Make About Joy

Most people think their joy comes from 1) people, 2) promotion, 3) progress, 4) power or 5) possessions. The wise person discovers the truth. The Holy Spirit creates joy within you every moment that He is pleasured.

▶ When you *pleasure Him through total obedience, you will feel what He is feeling.*

▶ When you *grieve Him and bring Him sorrow, you will feel what He is feeling.*

The Apostle Paul gave us an incredible photograph: "For the kingdom of God is not meat and drink; but righteousness, and peace, and joy in the Holy Ghost," (Romans 14:17).

The Holy Spirit will give you joy in the midst of

your most difficult and fiery trial. The apostles discovered this. After they were beaten, they kept their joy. "...and when they had called the apostles, and beaten them, they commanded that they should not speak in the name of Jesus, and let them go. And they departed from the presence of the council, rejoicing that they were counted worthy to suffer shame for His name," (Acts 5:40-41).

The joy of The Holy Spirit enables you to keep doing your Assignment in the midst of threats. "And daily in the temple, and in every house, they ceased not to teach and preach Jesus Christ," (Acts 5:42).

When The Holy Spirit controls your life, your words will become catalysts for blessing. "A man hath joy by the answer of his mouth: and a word spoken in due season, how good is it!" (Proverbs 15:23).

The Holy Spirit is your only true Source of peace.

Peace is the absence of inner conflict.

Inner battle is devastating. Sometimes, our conscience is at war against things we have done. Our focus on things greatly influences our emotions. If I analyze, evaluate and continuously think about injustices to me, my heart will become chaotic. My mind will become fragmented. My attitude will become critical.

The Holy Spirit resolves this inner turmoil.

The Fruit of The Holy Spirit is peace. "But the fruit of the Spirit is love, joy, PEACE, longsuffering, gentleness, goodness, faith, Meekness, temperance: against such there is no law," (Galatians 5:22-23).

You see, *His presence brings peace.* When you obey His instructions, a calmness will enter your spirit. The greatest warfare of your life is The Holy Spirit versus your flesh and self. "For the flesh lusteth against the Spirit, and the Spirit against the flesh: and these are contrary the one to the other: so that ye cannot do the things that ye would," (Galatians 5:17).

When you permit the leadership of The Holy Spirit in your life, you will enter the most remarkable and unforgettable season of calm and inner peace you could imagine.

- ▶ Man cannot give this peace.
- ▶ Popularity does not create this kind of peace.
- ▶ Wealth cannot produce this peace.
- ▶ Psychiatrists cannot produce this kind of peace.
- ▶ A loving mate does not produce this kind of peace.

Uncommon peace is a gift from an uncommon God. "And the peace of God, which passeth all understanding, shall keep your hearts and minds through Christ Jesus," (Philippians 4:7).

When you focus on The Holy Spirit, you develop the mind of Christ. "For to be carnally minded is death; but to be spiritually minded is life and peace," (Romans 8:6).

When The Holy Spirit becomes your focus, the storm in your mind begins to settle. You enter into the rest He promised. "This is the rest wherewith ye may cause the weary to rest; and this is the refreshing," (Isaiah 28:12).

The Holy Spirit must become your focus before you ever experience total and continuous peace. "Thou wilt keep him in perfect peace, whose mind is stayed on Thee: because he trusteth in Thee," (Isaiah 26:3).

3 Ways The Holy Spirit Affects Your Relationships

1. The Holy Spirit Will Give You Discernment Regarding Your Friendships. Some are contentious. Their fault-finding words create a climate of conflict, anger and cynicism. "...from such turn away," (2 Timothy 3:5). Mark people who carry a spirit of debate and strife. When The Holy Spirit is in leadership, you will discern them quickly. "But foolish and unlearned questions avoid, knowing that they do gender strifes," (2 Timothy 2:23).

2. The Holy Spirit Increases Your Patience With Others. This always brings peace when you interact with those you love. "And the servant of the Lord must not strive; but be gentle unto all men, apt to teach, patient," (2 Timothy 2:24). Unfortunately, most of us blame everyone around us for the climate of battle. However, battle requires two or more. If you refuse to fight, the war cannot continue. "Where no wood is, there the fire goeth out: so where there is no talebearer, the strife ceaseth. As coals are to burning coals, and wood to fire; so is a contentious man to kindle strife," (Proverbs 26:20-21).

3. The Holy Spirit Will Give You The Courage And Strength To Withdraw From The Company of Foolish People. This increases your peace. "Go from the presence of a foolish man, when thou perceiveth not in him the lips of knowledge," (Proverbs 14:7).

After a crusade one night, I was exceptionally joyful. Many had come to Christ. A good number had been healed. Everything was so peaceful. When several of us arrived at the restaurant, a staff person from the local church began to complain to the waitress. (A spot or something was on their glass.)

Within a few moments, everyone circulated their experiences of "roaches in food" and other unhappy and unfortunate experiences with restaurants during their lifetime. Within 30 minutes we went from a glorious move of The Holy Spirit to pessimism and despondency.

It came through the words of one person.

How sad! Remember this. You are a Door or a Wall. You can become a wall *against* cynicism, discouragement and pessimism. Or, you can be a door of entry for others to walk into joy. Oh, how I want to become the Door for the presence of God to enter. (Now, it is sometimes necessary to become a wall against things that are unholy, unrighteous and that bring unhappiness.)

3 Ways The Holy Spirit Uses The Word of God In Your Life

1.   The Word of God Is The Instrument of Peace For The Holy Spirit To Use. "Great peace have they which love Thy law: and nothing shall offend them," (Psalm 119:165).

2.   When The Word of God Is Sown Continuously In Your Heart, It Grows A Harvest of Peace. "Thou wilt keep him in perfect peace, whose mind is stayed on Thee: because he trusteth in Thee," (Isaiah 26:3). "How beautiful are the feet of them that preach the gospel of peace, and bring glad tidings of good things!" (Romans 10:15).

3.   You Must Embrace The Word of God As

The Most Effective Instrument For Change. "All scripture is given by inspiration of God, and is profitable for doctrine, for reproof, for correction, for instruction in righteousness: That the man of God may be perfect, throughly furnished unto all good works," (2 Timothy 3:16-17).

When someone approaches me in great emotional havoc and disturbance, I know that The Word of God is not dominating their life. They discuss their battles instead of the One who is fighting for them.

5 Signs That Someone Is Not Word-Conscious

1. They Discuss Their Warfare, Instead of The Promise of Victory.

2. They Discuss Their Doubts, Instead of Their Faith In God.

3. Their Focus Is Their Enemy, Instead of Their Comforter.

4. If The Word of God Were Dominating Their Mind, It Would Dominate Their Mouth.

5. If The Word Dominated Their Mind, It Would Influence Their Conduct And Behavior.

▶ The Holy Spirit *inspired the Scriptures.*

▶ The Holy Spirit affects your *words.*

▶ The Holy Spirit *uses The Word of God* to bring peace into your heart. Do not throw it away. Do not treat it lightly.

4 Tips For Creating A Peaceful Climate

1. Recognize That Conflict Is The Trap For Distraction. Satan uses conflict to break your focus on your Assignment. Have you ever wondered, after an argument with someone, why they have focused on such trivia? It did not make sense. Some have forfeited a 20-year friendship or marriage, because of one sentence spoken in a day. That is demonic. It is satanic. It is not even logical. The purpose was to break your focus on things that are worthy.

That is why the Apostle Paul wrote to the church at Philippi, "And the peace of God, which passeth all understanding, shall keep your hearts and minds through Christ Jesus...whatsoever things are true... honest...just...pure...lovely...of good report...think on these things," (Philippians 4:7-8).

2.   You Determine Your Own Focus. Nobody else can. You can complain. You can blame others. But, you are responsible for what you give your attention to. *Your focus is creating your feelings.* Whatever you are feeling is produced by your focus.

▶ Your focus is *your* personal decision.

▶ Stop and take time to *change* your focus.

3.   Pay Any Price To Protect Your Focus On Right Things. "And if thy hand offend thee, cut it off: it is better for thee to enter into life maimed, than having two hands to go into hell, into the fire that never shall be quenched:...And if thine eye offend thee, pluck it out: it is better for thee to enter into the kingdom of God with one eye, than having two eyes to be cast into hell fire," (Mark 9:43, 47). "Thou wilt keep him in perfect peace, whose mind is stayed on Thee," (Isaiah 26:3).

"But now in Christ Jesus ye who sometimes were far off are made nigh by the blood of Christ. For He is our peace, who hath made both one, and hath broken down the middle wall of partition between us; Having abolished in His flesh the enmity, even the law of commandments contained in ordinances; for to make in Himself of twain one new man, so making peace; And that He might reconcile both unto God in one body by the cross, having slain the enmity thereby: And came and preached peace to you which were afar off, and to them that were nigh," (Ephesians 2:13-17).

"These things I have spoken unto you, that in Me ye might have peace. In the world ye shall have tribulation: but be of good cheer; I have overcome the world," (John 16:33).

4.   **The Holy Spirit Is Your True Source of Love.** Love Is The Most Powerful Force On Earth. The Holy Spirit Is The Source of The Greatest Force On Earth—Love. "...because the love of God is shed abroad in our hearts by the Holy Ghost which is given unto us," (Romans 5:5).

15 Facts About Holy Spirit Love

1.   **The Fruit of The Holy Spirit Is Love.** "But the fruit of the Spirit is love," (Galatians 5:22). It is The Holy Spirit that places an unexplainable love within a mother's heart for her child; the husband's heart for his wife; the pastor's heart for his people.

2.   **The Proof of Love Is The Desire To Give.** "For God so loved the world, that He gave His only begotten Son, that whosoever believeth in Him should not perish, but have everlasting life," (John 3:16). God *gave.* That *proved* His love.

3.   **The Holy Spirit Enabled Jesus To Love.** He prayed, "Father, forgive them; for they know not

what they do," (Luke 23:34).

4. The Holy Spirit Enabled Stephen To Love Those Who Stoned Him. "And he kneeled down, and cried with a loud voice, Lord, lay not this sin to their charge," (Acts 7:60).

The Holy Spirit alone could plant this kind of love inside a human heart. It would have been normal to pray a prayer that called down fire from Heaven on those stoning you. This is a remarkable work of grace in the human heart. It is normal to retaliate. It is human to fight back. It is uncommon and Divine to forgive. This is true love.

5. The Love of Christ Enables Missionaries To Fight Emotional Battles, Financial Difficulties And Cultural Barriers In Their Ministry Among Heathen. I have lived with missionaries. Some have forfeited the comforts and luxury of home to empty their lives into a small village. Why? The love of Christ, placed there by *The Holy Spirit,* for unlovable people.

6. Many Wives Have Birthed The Salvation of Their Husbands Because of The Love of The Holy Spirit Within Them. Their husbands came to Christ because of their conversation and conduct. They never quit loving their husbands.

7. Thousands of Rebellious Teenagers Have Been Drawn Back Home Like A Magnet To A Loving Parent Because of The Love of The Holy Spirit. Certainly, parents have felt discouraged and demoralized. Anger is common among disappointed parents. But, The Holy Spirit can do the impossible— impart an uncommon love for a rebellious and stubborn teenager.

8. God Sends His Love Toward You Even In The Worse Season of Your Life. "But God commendeth His love toward us, in that, while we were yet sinners, Christ died for us," (Romans 5:8).

9. Love Pursues. "For the Son of man is come to seek and to save that which was lost," (Luke 19:10). (See also John 3:16 and Isaiah 1:18.)

10. Love Protects. "...for I the Lord thy God am a jealous God," (Exodus 20:5).

11. Love Provides. "...for I am the Lord that healeth thee," (Exodus 15:26). Here is a song I wrote to The Holy Spirit some time ago:

Love Words

Make all my words—Your love words.
Make all my words—Your love words.
That's what You've made me for, Holy Spirit,
To pour Your healing oil.
Make all my words—Your love words.

12. The Love of The Holy Spirit Is Not Manipulating Another.

13. The Love of The Holy Spirit Is Not Decided By The Conduct And Behavior of Another.

14. Love Will Never Cease. *Paul understood this.* "Now he that planteth and he that watereth are one: and every man shall receive his own reward according to his own labour. For we are labourers together with God: ye are God's husbandry, ye are God's building. According to the grace of God which is given unto me, as a wise masterbuilder, I have laid the foundation, and another buildeth thereon. But let every man take heed how he buildeth thereupon. Every man's work shall be made manifest: for the day shall declare it, because it shall be revealed by fire; and the fire shall try every man's work of what sort it is," (1 Corinthians 3:8-10, 13).

15. The Love of The Holy Spirit Dissolves Fear. "There is no fear in love; but perfect love casteth out fear: because fear hath torment. He that feareth is not made perfect in love," (1 John 4:18).

Our Prayer Together...
"Father, thank You for the promise of peace. The world is in battle. Every day is an emotional war. Everything around me seems designed to break my focus and create distraction. But, Your Word is a lamp unto my feet and a light unto my path. Because I love Thy Word, my peace is great. Holy Spirit, You are the true Source of peace. You are The Spirit of peace, and I embrace You today. Your words matter to me. Thank You for The Word of God, the Instrument of Peace, that You have given to me. It drives out darkness and brings me into a place of rest. In Jesus' name. Amen."

∽ 5 ∽
THE HOLY SPIRIT IS GRIEVED BY WRONG CONVERSATION AND CONDUCT

The Holy Spirit Is Holy.

Words matter to Him. Conversation is important to Him. Your conduct and behavior is monitored continuously.

17 Facts Every Christian Should Know About Grieving The Holy Spirit

1.   The Holy Spirit Is Easily Grieved And Offended. That is why the Apostle Paul wrote this remarkable warning: "Let no corrupt communication proceed out of your mouth, but that which is good to the use of edifying, that it may minister grace unto the hearers. *And grieve not the Holy Spirit of God*, whereby ye are sealed unto the day of redemption. Let all bitterness, and wrath, and anger, and clamour, and evil speaking, be put away from you, with all malice: And be ye kind one to another, tenderhearted, forgiving one another, even as God for Christ's sake hath forgiven you," (Ephesians 4:29-32).

2.   He Will Withdraw His Manifest Presence When He Has Been Grieved And Offended. "I will go and return to My place, till they acknowledge their offence, and seek My face: in their affliction they will seek Me early," (Hosea 5:15).

3.   You Must Permit The Holy Spirit To Correct You When You Have Offended Him. Any words that *wound* the *influence* of *someone not present* are *disloyal words*. Disloyalty is unholy. It is so important that you permit The Holy Spirit to correct you and prevent you from saying anything that is grievous to Him. His presence must be valued. His presence brings joy, peace and calmness in spirit. You cannot afford a day without His presence.

4.   The Holy Spirit Is The Reason You Should Avoid Accusatory And Unflattering Conversation About Others. He withdraws! His absence creates sorrow and heaviness of spirit. "Let the words of my mouth, and the meditation of my heart, be acceptable in Thy sight, O Lord, my strength, and my redeemer," (Psalm 19:14).

Oh, please do not grieve The Holy Spirit! Whatever the cost! Whatever it takes, do not offend the One Who Stayed.

The love of God has been so misunderstood. His mercy has been taken for granted by millions.

"Oh, well! God knows my heart," laughed one lady when her pastor asked her why she had not been to church in several months. She had been taking vacations, spending her time out on the lake on Sundays. Yet, she had become so accustomed to ignoring the inner voice of The Holy Spirit, her conscience had become seared and numb.

5.   It Is A Dangerous Moment To Assume That Access To The Holy Spirit Is Frivolous or Permanent. Oh, treasure His Presence today! His Presence keeps you *soft* toward Him. His Presence keeps you hungry and thirsty. When you do not pursue His Presence, the danger of becoming calloused and hardened is very real. A minister once told me, "I never dreamed I could get this far from God." As I looked at Him, I was shocked. Here sat a man who had preached with fire in His soul, love pouring through his heart, many years before.

But, he had offended The Holy Spirit. Over and over again. Now, The Holy Spirit had withdrawn from Him. He had even *lost* his hunger and his thirst for the presence of God.

When you feel troubled in your spirit, thank God for such a troubling! Millions have ignored Him so long that the fire of desire has died out. Only ashes remain.

6. There Are Seasons For Repentance Provided By The Holy Spirit. *Jesus wept over Jerusalem.* "O Jerusalem, Jerusalem, thou that killest the prophets, and stonest them which are sent unto thee, how often would I have gathered thy children together, even as a hen gathereth her chickens under her wings, and ye would not!" (Matthew 23:37).

7. The Presence of God Yesterday Does Not Guarantee The Presence of God Tomorrow. Look at what happened to Saul. He had known the anointing. God selected him. God touched his life. The prophet of God anointed him. Yet, "...the Spirit of the Lord departed from Saul, and an evil spirit from the Lord troubled him," (1 Samuel 16:14).

He died the death of a fool.

8. Great Men Dread The Horror of The Absence of The Holy Spirit. *The psalmist knew the terrifying seasons when The Holy Spirit seemed withdrawn from him.* David had been with Saul. He experienced evil spirits departing as he played his harp. He saw the touch of God on Saul come and *leave.* He cried out after his terrible sin with Bathsheba, "Cast me not away from Thy presence; and take not Thy Holy Spirit from me," (Psalm 51:11). Now, theologians laugh at David's confession and pursuit. Thousands of ministers say David was wrong, that The Holy Spirit could not withdraw from him. (Don't kid yourself. He had observed King Saul's deterioration before his own eyes.)

9. Every Seasoned Minister Has Encountered Someone Who No Longer Experiences The Deep Wooing of The Holy Spirit. If you have spent much time with people, as a minister of the gospel, you will meet many from whom The Holy Spirit has appeared to have withdrawn His pulling and drawing. No, He does not do it easily or quickly. He is longsuffering. He is patient.

But, repeated rejection of His drawing has devastating results.

10. Emptiness Occurs After You Have Grieved The Holy Spirit. The Song of Solomon contains one of the saddest photographs of love rejected and lost. "I opened to my beloved; but my beloved had withdrawn Himself, and was gone: my soul failed when He spake, I sought Him, but I could not find Him; I called Him but He gave me no answer," (Song of Solomon 5:6).

11. Rejection of Him Always Produces Desolation. "Behold, your house is left unto you desolate," (Matthew 23:38).

12. Rejection of The Holy Spirit Can Be Fatal. Jesus said it clearly, "Remember Lot's wife,"

(Luke 17:32). The angels had appeared personally to escort Lot and his family from danger to safety. But, she took it lightly. Their instructions became unimportant. She rebelled and did what she desired. She became a pillar of salt.

13. Satan Often Lies To Someone About The Withdrawing of The Holy Spirit. He makes them feel that it is useless to pray, futile to reach and hopeless to believe for a change. Satan often tells people that they have sinned "the unpardonable sin" when the opposite is true.

Most have never read these terrifying words in Hosea 5:15: "I will go and return to My place, till they acknowledge their offence, and seek My face: in their affliction they will seek Me early."

14. Restoration Is Possible After You Have Offended The Holy Spirit. I raise my voice with Hosea today: "Come, and let us return unto the Lord: for He hath torn, and He will heal us; He hath smitten, and He will bind us up. After two days will He revive us: in the third day He will raise us up, and we shall live in His sight. Then shall we know, if we follow on to know the Lord," (Hosea 6:1-3).

15. If You Have A Deep Desire For God, The Holy Spirit Is Still At Work. That is how you know if you have not sinned the unpardonable sin! The Father is the One who draws you. If you still have within your heart a sincere desire to know God and an appetite to pursue Him, you have not yet sinned the unpardonable sin. You see, only God can draw you. *If He is* drawing you, it is not too late.

You still have a chance for a miraculous *experience* with Him.

16. Treasure The Drawing Toward The Holy Spirit Today As A Gift From Your Heavenly Father. "No man can come to Me, except the Father which hath sent Me draw him: and I will raise him up at the last day. It is written in the prophets, And they shall be all taught of God," (John 6:44-45).

17. Conversation Can Grieve The Holy Spirit. "Let no corrupt communication proceed out of your mouth, but that which is good to the use of edifying, that it may minister grace unto the hearers. And grieve not the holy Spirit of God, whereby ye are sealed unto the day of redemption," (Ephesians 4:29-30).

I will never forget a conversation in Washington, DC. I came down from my hotel room full of joy and enthusiasm. I had been praying in the Spirit throughout the day. I could not remember happier hours or days in my life. When I sat down to eat, the name of someone came up. I was talking with two of my staff members. When this name came up, I made a statement: "I like him, but he is rather lazy." The conversation continued. After about one hour, I returned to my hotel room again.

But something was wrong. Something had changed since I had gone to supper! As I began to lift my hands and sing to The Holy Spirit, a cloud of heaviness and a shadow on my heart appeared. Something was *out of order.* So not really knowing yet what was wrong, I simply began to sing louder and become more aggressive in my worship.

Yet, the heaviness in my spirit continued. Suddenly, The Holy Spirit spoke to my heart: "Why did you tell them that this young man was lazy?"

I stopped. Then I replied almost defiantly to The Holy Spirit—"Well, because he *is* lazy!"

"You have offended Me," The Holy Spirit spoke into my heart.

I thought for a moment. Then I replied: "Well, he did not hear me anyway. He is over 1,000 miles away!"

"I heard you, and *you offended Me.*"

I tried another approach. "Well, Lord, it is true that he is lazy, and I would tell him to his face!"

Suddenly, The Holy Spirit stopped me. He brought my mind back to Philippians 4:8 where He gave us the criteria and guidelines for proper conversation "whatsoever things are..."

- ▶ True.
- ▶ Honest.
- ▶ Just.
- ▶ Pure.
- ▶ Lovely.
- ▶ Good report.
- ▶ Virtuous.
- ▶ Things that are praiseworthy.

As He began to deal with my life, my heart began to break. I saw that I had spoken in a *destructive* way about someone *who was precious to Him.*

Thoughts that do not qualify for *meditation*, do not qualify for *conversation*. If it does not qualify for my mind, it did not qualify for my mouth.

Picture a mother showing you a photograph of her baby. Can you imagine her response to you if you began to sneer and make fun of her child! "What an ugly child. I despise that child!" That mother would withdraw from you instantly.

Yet, it happens in your own life every day. The

moment you begin to discuss the flaws of *those not present*—The Holy Spirit *withdraws*.

A few weeks later, one of my staff members approached me. I asked the purpose of the appointment. She was upset with another staff member.

"Then, let's call her and have her to hear your accusation against her," I reached for the telephone. "I really would grieve The Holy Spirit if I discuss the flaws of someone not present, unable to defend themselves."

"Never mind, then! I don't want her to hear what I'm saying! Let's just forget about it."

Imagine if every church congregation would focus for 12 months on proper conversation about others. Imagine what your home would be like if every family member would only speak well of each other.

You see, we have been taught to avoid saying bad about people *because—they may find out about it.* Oh, my precious friend, that is not the only reason to avoid wrong conversation. Others warn, "What goes around will come back around." That, too, is not the right reason for avoiding destructive words about others.

⚜ **6** ⚜
THE HOLY SPIRIT INTERCEDES FOR YOU CONTINUOUSLY

Somebody Is Praying For You Right Now.

18 Facts Every Believer Should Know About Intercession

1. **The Holy Spirit Is On Earth Interceding For You To The Father.** "He maketh intercession for the saints according to the will of God," (Romans 8:27).

So, there is an incredible and beautiful scenario of intercession occurring 24-hours-a-day, every day of your life.

You may *feel* alone. You may *feel* isolated. You may even have tormenting thoughts that nobody really cares for you at all. But, the opposite is occurring. The Holy Spirit continuously talks to the Father about your needs and desires.

While you are asleep, He is praying for you.

While you are working, He is praying for you.

When you have doubts, He is praying for you.

2. **Jesus Is In Heaven Praying For You Also.** "It is Christ that died, yea rather, that is risen again, Who is even at the right hand of God, Who also maketh intercession for us," (Romans 8:34).

3. **You Truly Are The Apple of Your Father's Eye.** "For the Lord's portion is His people; Jacob is the lot of His inheritance. He found him in a desert land, and in the waste howling wilderness; He led him about, He instructed him, He kept him as the apple of His eye," (Deuteronomy 32:9-10).

4. Your Father Has Committed Himself To Your Protection. "As an eagle stirreth up her nest, fluttereth over her young, spreadeth abroad her wings, taketh them, beareth them on her wings: So the Lord alone did lead him, and there was no strange God with him," (Deuteronomy 32:11-12).

5. Your Father Wants You To Experience Uncommon Success And Provision. "He made him ride on the high places of the earth, that he might eat the increase of the fields; and He made him to suck honey out of the rock, and oil out of the flinty rock; Butter of kine, and milk of sheep, with fat of lambs, and rams of the breed of Bashan, and goats, with the fat of kidneys of wheat; and thou didst drink the pure blood of the grape," (Deuteronomy 32:13-14).

6. You Cannot Even Imagine The Magnitude And Greatness of God's Desires For You. That is why our prayers are often ineffective, incomplete and unanswered. "Eye hath not see, nor ear heard, neither have entered into the heart of man, the things which God hath prepared for them that love him," (1 Corinthians 2:9).

7. The Holy Spirit Has Searched Out, Pho-tographed, Inventoried And Documented The Desires of The Father Toward You. "But God hath revealed them unto us by His Spirit: for the Spirit searcheth all things, yea the deep things of God," (1 Corinthians 2:10).

8. The Holy Spirit Is The Only Person In

The Universe Who Knows The Heart of The Father. "For what man knoweth the things of a man, save the spirit of man which is in him? even so the things of God knoweth no man, but the Spirit of God," (1 Corinthians 2:11).

9.   The Holy Spirit Is Given To Us To Reveal The Desires of The Father Toward Us. "Now we have received, not the spirit of the world, but the Spirit which is of God; that we might know the things that are freely given to us of God," (1 Corinthians 2:12).

10. Your Natural Man (The Self Life) Continuously Rejects The Things of The Holy Spirit. "But the natural man receiveth not the things of the Spirit of God: for they are foolishness unto him: neither can he know them, because they are spiritually discerned," (1 Corinthians 2:14).

11. Humans Simply Do Not Know How To Pray Effectively In A Way That Pleases The Heart of God. "For we know not what we should pray for as we ought," (Romans 8:26).

12. The Holy Spirit Is Our Committed Personal Intercessor Every Day. "Likewise the Spirit also helpeth our infirmities...but the Spirit itself maketh intercession for us with groanings which cannot be uttered," (Romans 8:26).

13. The Holy Spirit Is In Total Agreement With The Desires And Will of The Father For You. "And He that searcheth the hearts knoweth what is the mind of the Spirit, because He maketh intercession for the saints according to the will of God," (Romans 8:27).

14. The Holy Spirit Is Passionate About Your Needs And Desires Being Fulfilled. "...but the Spirit itself maketh intercession for us with *groanings* *which cannot be uttered,"* (Romans 8:26).

15. The Holy Spirit Stirs Others To Intercede For You, Too. He did this in Samuel's heart for the people of God. "Moreover as for me, God forbid that I should sin against the Lord in ceasing to pray for you: but I will teach you the good and the right way," (1 Samuel 12:23). The Apostle Paul experienced the same kind of stirring to intercession by The Holy Spirit. His protégé, Timothy, received this word from his mentor. "I thank God, whom I serve from my forefathers with pure conscience, that without ceasing I have remembrance of thee in my prayers night and day," (2 Timothy 1:3).

16. You Are Never Alone In The Storms of Your Life. Ever. Jesus promised it. "And I will pray the Father, and He shall give you another Comforter, that He may abide with you for ever," (John 14:16).

Your *success* is not limited to your *efforts alone*.

Your *future* is not controlled by *just your personal knowledge only*.

Your *victories* are *not* dependent on your personal abilities *alone*.

17. The Holy Spirit And Jesus Are Your Personal Intercessors Throughout Every Trial And Difficult Place of Your Life. That is why the Apostle Paul could shout with joy and thanksgiving in the midst of the most difficult, cold, damp prison experiences: "Who shall separate us from the love of Christ? shall tribulation, or distress, or persecution, or famine, or nakedness, or peril, or sword?...Nay, in all these things we are more than conquerors through Him that loved us. For I am persuaded, that neither death, nor life, nor angels, nor principalities, nor powers, nor things present, nor things to come, Nor height, nor depth, nor any other creature, shall be able to separate us from the love of God, which is in Christ Jesus our Lord," (Romans 8:35, 37-39).

18. Your Survival Is Guaranteed Because Someone Is Interceding For You. "Wherefore He is able also to save them to the uttermost that come unto God by Him, seeing He ever liveth to make intercession for them," (Hebrews 7:25).

Our Prayer Together...

"Precious Father, thank You for hearing my prayers today. You always respond to the cries of my heart. Thank You most of all for hearing the intercessions of my precious Comforter, The Holy Spirit, every day of my life. Thank You for receiving the prayers of Jesus, the One who died for me. Today, I will enthusiastically live in peace and in joy every moment because You will answer the prayers of those who are interceding for me. I am so thankful also, Father, that You are stirring other men and women of God to call my name before Your throne. You are imparting faith, hope and have promised total victory. I accept it, in Jesus' name. Amen."

❧ Psalm 100:2 ❧

"Come before His Presence with singing."

⇜ 7 ⇝

THE HOLY SPIRIT LOVES SINGING

Singing Is Very Important To The Holy Spirit.

17 Facts Every Christian Should Know About Singing To The Holy Spirit

1. God Sings Over You As Well. "The Lord thy God in the midst of thee is mighty; He will save, He will rejoice over thee with joy; He will rest in His love, *He will joy over thee with singing,*" (Zephaniah 3:17).

Many people cannot imagine our God singing. But, He does! I can picture this so clearly in my heart. The Holy Spirit is like a mother leaning over the bed of her small child and singing, "Sleep, my precious baby! Sleep, precious love of my life. I will watch over you and protect you."

2. The Holy Spirit Wants You To Sing When You Enter His Presence. "...come before His presence with singing," (Psalm 100:2).

Sounds are wonderful to The Holy Spirit! Listen to the birds today as they sing out in wonderment! Listen to the sounds of animals, the wind blowing through the trees and even the wonderful love sounds of those family members close to you. Singing is an essential part of their world. Likewise, The Holy Spirit wants you to be aware of His fervent desire to hear you sing to

Him!

3. Focus Your Singing To The Holy Spirit, Instead of People. I have written over 5,000 songs throughout my lifetime. Yet, the songs I love to sing the most are the Love Songs to The Holy Spirit. I call them, "Songs From The Secret Place." Hundreds of songs have been birthed in my heart since I fell in love with The Holy Spirit on Wednesday, July 13, 1994, at 7:00 a.m.

4. Sing From Your Heart, Not Your Mind. He does not need unusual words, an unorthodox philosophy or beautiful sounds. He simply wants you to open your heart and let the "love sounds" flow from you. (Read 1 Corinthians 13.)

5. Sing To The Holy Spirit In Your Prayer Language, Too. The Apostle Paul understood the incredible power of singing. "I will sing with the spirit, and I will sing with the understanding also," (1 Corinthians 14:15).

6. Singing Is A Weapon God Has Used To Birth Uncommon Events. Prison doors have been opened miraculously when singing and worship occurred. "And at midnight Paul and Silas prayed, and sang praises unto God," (Acts 16:25).

7. The Holy Spirit Wants You To Sing Together With Other Saints. "Speaking to yourselves in psalms and hymns and spiritual songs, singing and making melody in your heart to the Lord," (Ephesians 5:19).

8. When You Sing To The Holy Spirit, Evil Spirits Will Leave. King Saul discovered this under the ministry of David. In fact, the music of David *refreshed* Saul. "And it came to pass, when the evil spirit from God was upon Saul, that David took an harp, and played with his hand: so Saul was refreshed, and was well, and the evil spirit departed from him," (1 Samuel 16:23).

9. Singers Were An Essential Part of Battles In The Old Testament. Listen to the conduct of Jehoshaphat. "And when he had consulted with the people, he appointed singers unto the Lord, and that should praise the beauty of holiness, as they went out before the army, and to say, Praise the Lord; for His mercy endureth for ever," (2 Chronicles 20:21).

10. Singers Were Often The Reason For Victories Against The Enemies of God. "And when they began to sing and to praise, the Lord set ambushments against the children of Ammon, Moab, and mount Seir, which were come against Judah; and they were smitten," (2 Chronicles 20:22).

11. Your Singing Is A Weapon. Read again the incredible story of Paul and Silas in prison. Everything was going against them. They had been beaten. They were alone and in incredible pain. But, they understood the *Weapon of Singing.* "And at midnight Paul and Silas prayed, and sang praises unto God: and the prisoners heard them. And suddenly there was a great earthquake, so that the foundations of the prison were shaken: and immediately all the doors were opened, and every one's bands were loosed," (Acts 16:25-26). The foundations, the very things that cause their captivity—were destroyed...*as they began to sing.*

12. Singing Can Make Your Enemy Demoralized, Discouraged And Decide To Move Away From You. Paul watched this happen when he and Silas sang in the prison. "And the keeper of the prison awaking out of his sleep, and seeing the prison doors open, he drew out his sword, and would have killed himself, supposing that the prisoners had been fled," (Acts 16:27).

13. Your Singing May Be The Turning Point In Someone's Personal Salvation. It happened for the jailer when Paul and Silas sang. "Then he called for a light, and sprang in, and came trembling, and fell down before Paul and Silas, And brought them out, and said, Sirs, what must I do to be saved?" (Acts 16:29-30).

14. Moses, The Great Leader, Understood The Heart of God About Singing. After Israel saw Pharaoh's army destroyed, they sang. "Then sang Moses and the children of Israel this song unto the Lord, and spake, saying, I will sing unto the Lord, for He hath triumphed gloriously: the horse and His rider hath He thrown into the sea," (Exodus 15:1).

15. Deborah, The Great Prophetess, Understood How To Express Appreciation of God Through Singing. After the defeat of Sisera and Jabin, she honored the Lord. "Then sang Deborah and Barak...Praise ye the Lord for the avenging of Israel, when the people willingly offered themselves. Hear, O ye kings; give ear, O ye princes; I, even I, will sing unto the Lord; I will sing praise to the Lord God of Israel," (Judges 5:1-3).

16. Singing Often Precedes The Flow of Miracles In Significant Healing Ministries. Sometimes, I have sat for two to 3 hours before the miracles and healings began. Songs that honored The Holy Spirit and the greatness of God always seem to unlock faith into the atmosphere. He always comes when He is celebrated and honored. You see, He instructed us how to approach Him—come with singing. (Read Psalm 100:2.)

17. Your Singing Is An Act of Obedience To The Holy Spirit. "Serve the Lord with gladness: come before His presence with singing," (Psalm 100:2).

That is why I placed 24 speakers on the trees in my 7-acre yard. I cannot tell you how wonderful it is to walk across my yard, hearing these songs to The Holy Spirit. I have installed speakers throughout the rooms of my home, playing songs to The Holy Spirit continuously. Words cannot describe the effect it has in your heart and mind. In fact, recently when some of my CD's (compact discs) were damaged, it seemed like death replaced life around my house! *The Holy Spirit comes when He is celebrated.*

Invest in an excellent, quality stereo and make music a major part of every day. It is worth every penny. Your mind will respond. Your heart will find new fire. Your body will receive a surging of new energy and vitality. Most of all, The Holy Spirit will manifest His presence.

4 Wonderful Things That Happen When You Sing

► Your singing to The Holy Spirit *will create an atmosphere of thanksgiving.*

► Your singing will greatly *influence your focus.*

► Your singing will dispel *every demonic influence assigned to distract you.*

► Your singing will arouse the energy and passion of your own body to focus on the Creator.

Singing can change everything around your life. Everything. So, begin this very moment. Close this book and begin to sing *aloud* to The Holy Spirit. Your words may be simple, but they will become powerful. "I love You, Holy Spirit!

I love You, Holy Spirit!

I love You, Holy Spirit!

You are good, so good to me!" So, you and I can learn from the champions. Those who have conquered in battle had discerned the hidden and mysterious power of singing. You must do it in your own life today! "Saying, I will declare Thy name unto my brethren, in the midst of the church will I sing praise unto Thee," (Hebrews 2:12).

Our Prayer Together...

"Father, thank You for revealing the weapon of singing to my life. I will sing...when things go wrong or right. I will sing *regardless of my circumstances.* I will sing for the purpose of *honoring You* and *obeying You!* I will sing *songs of remembrance,* because I remember every blessing You have given me! I will sing *continuously,* knowing that as I sing, angels come and minister to me! I will sing with *victory,* knowing that demonic spirits that hear my words are becoming fragmented and confused. I will sing, knowing that my mouth is my *Deliverer!* I will teach *my children* to sing to You! Thank You for *singing to me,* over my life! In Jesus' name. Amen."

RECOMMENDED INVESTMENTS:
The Wisdom Commentary, Vol. 2 (Book/B-220/312 pgs)
Love Songs To The Holy Spirit, Series 1 (CD/CDS-59)
Love Songs To The Holy Spirit, Series 2 (CD/CDS-61)

∽ 8 ∽
THE HOLY SPIRIT CAN PROVIDE YOU WITH A PRAYER LANGUAGE THAT NOBODY UNDERSTANDS BUT GOD

———————————

Your Prayer Language Is Very Important.

While millions have never understood this wonderful and glorious experience, thousands of others are tasting this incredible phenomenon—"praying in the Heavenly language." It is not as confusing as it may first appear.

9 Facts You Should Know About Tongues And Your Prayer Life

1. The Creator Is A Communicator. He provided animals sounds to create connections between themselves. The wildest animals on earth even communicate with each other.

2. Relationship Is The Goal And Focus of The Holy Spirit. He provided every nationality a language of their own. The Spanish have their language. The French have their language. The Germans have their language. The English have their language and even animals signal to their own continually.

3. The One Who Gives Languages On Earth

Simply Has One of His Own. Most of us call it *"The Heavenly Language."* "For he that speaketh in an unknown tongue speaketh not unto men, but unto God: for no man understandeth him," (1 Corinthians 14:2).

4.   There Are Varied Uses of This Heavenly Language That Are Rewarding And Apply To Different Situations. For example, when The Holy Spirit came on the day of Pentecost, He provided a language that was unknown only to those who were speaking it! Others *around them* understood! The Holy Spirit was simply providing an opportunity for the gospel to be heard *in other dialects.* "...the multitude came together, and were confounded, because that every man heard them speak in his own language. And they were all amazed and marvelled, saying one to another, Behold, are not all these which speak Galileans? And how hear we every man in our own tongue, wherein we were born?" (Acts 2:6-8).

Yet, Peter and the others who were speaking "in tongues," did not understand what was coming from their own lips. This was *not* the Heavenly language, but rather The Holy Spirit using a language or dialect to confirm His message to them.

5.   So, God Often Uses Varying Ways To Use "Unknown Tongues" To Impress Unbelievers About A Supernatural God. "Wherefore tongues are for a sign, not to them that believe, but to them that believe not," (1 Corinthians 14:22).

6.   The Holy Spirit Is Meticulous And Orderly In The Plan of How And When Tongues Are Used. Sometimes, when followed by an interpretation, tongues are used to bless the entire church so the people can be edified and blessed. "Wherefore let him that speaketh in an unknown tongue pray that he may interpret," (1 Corinthians 14:13).

7. The Holy Spirit Will Often Pray Through You In Private Intercession "Through Tongues" For Others. "Likewise the Spirit also helpeth our infirmities: for we know not what we should pray for as we ought: but the Spirit itself maketh intercession for us with groanings which cannot be uttered. And He that searcheth the hearts knoweth what is the mind of the Spirit, because He maketh intercession for the saints according to the will of God," (Romans 8:26-27).

8. When You Pray "In Tongues," You Increase And Build Yourself Up And Your Personal Faith And Confidence In God. Something supernatural occurs. It is indescribable, unexplainable and undeniable. "But ye, beloved, building up yourselves on your most holy faith, praying in the Holy Ghost, Keep yourselves in the love of God, looking for the mercy of our Lord Jesus Christ unto eternal life," (Jude 1:20-21). This is essential for overcomers. You see, *your victories depend on your faith.* Faith is confidence in God. It is the *only way* to bring pleasure to God. "But without faith it is impossible to please Him: for He that cometh to God must believe that He is, and that He is a rewarder of them that diligently seek Him," (Hebrews 11:6).

9. It Is Important For You To Keep Your Prayer Language Alive And Vibrant. "I thank my God, I speak with tongues more than ye all," (1 Corinthians 14:18).

I have had unforgettable experiences with my prayer language: I experienced the baptism of The Holy Spirit and "speaking with tongues" at the age of 10. My second dramatic encounter was at about the age of 15 in Beaumont, Texas.

I have always prayed in The Holy Spirit, even from my early youth. But, I have never understood the practice of "interpreting back in English what The Holy Spirit had spoken through me to the Father."

Oral Roberts brought me into a special understanding of this.

I was in a huge conference at the Mabee Center in Tulsa, Oklahoma. After the service one day, Oral Roberts walked over to me and asked me to go with him to his office. There, he began to tell me the secrets behind the remarkable blessings of God on his ministry and work.

"The two keys to everything accomplished for God have been: 1) Seed-faith and 2) Praying in The Spirit," he explained.

"Mike, God has shown you more about the principle of Seed-faith than any man I've ever known in my life, but I'd like to tell you about *praying in The Spirit and interpreting back in tongues.*"

Well, this seemed a little strange to me. But, I knew that the hand of God was strong in his life. He has been a wonderful mentor in my life that I value and celebrate. I listened. *Uncommon Experiences Create Uncommon Men.*

He explained that after praying in The Spirit (in tongues), I should ask The Holy Spirit and be willing to trust Him to provide me the interpretation in my own language, English. (Then, I could plan and prepare my life according to what The Holy Spirit had been praying for me.)

"But," I protested, "what if something comes out of

my mouth that is crazy, illogical and ridiculous?"

"Trust The Holy Spirit," he said gently.

The next morning, I arose at 5:30, my prayer time. (I was scheduled to meet with a realtor at 9:30 and purchase an office building in Tulsa. Someone was giving me a ride at 9:00 to the appointment. My manager had been selected, and several houses were being purchased for my staff.) As I began to pray in the Spirit, suddenly, I began to pray in English. It burst out of my mouth suddenly and unexpectedly: *"This day will not go as you have planned. But, do not fear—it is My Will."*

I felt odd, a little peculiar, but aware that I was moving into a different realm than normal.

At 9:00, my ride appeared. Within 30 minutes, some unexpected things occurred. Statements were made, and things happened beyond my control. The purchase of the building was canceled. The houses for my staff were canceled. The peace of God came into me to stay in Dallas instead of moving to Tulsa. It was shocking. Yet, as I replayed my prayer time at 5:30 that morning, The Holy Spirit had told me in English that the day would not go as I had planned.

Paul understood this.

"What is it then? I will pray with the Spirit, and I will pray with the understanding also," (1 Corinthians 14:15).

I had two other unusual encounters with my prayer language in my Secret Place at home. As I was praying fervently in tongues, suddenly I burst out in English these words:

"Expose fraudulent people in my life! Holy Spirit, expose fraudulent people in my life!"

I could hardly believe what was coming from my mouth. Fraudulent people? I did not know any fraudulent people around my life. I trusted everyone close to me explicitly. I have always felt very discerning and that I could "pick up anything wrong." But, The Holy Spirit knew something I did not know. *He knows the hearts of others many years before you do.*

I had turned my personal finances over to a long-time friend. I trusted this friend more than any human on earth. Yet, within 7 days I discovered this friend had written checks for thousands of dollars unauthorized and without my permission. It was shocking, unsettling and disheartening. But, The Holy Spirit had helped prepare my heart. He was talking to the Father in my behalf. When I interpreted in English what He was praying through me (in tongues), it became a spiritual milestone in my memory.

Since then, I have trusted The Holy Spirit to pray anything He desires, knowing that *He wants only that which is good for me*. "...no good thing will he withhold from them that walk uprightly," (Psalm 84:11).

A few days later, another uncommon event occurred. As I was praying in the Spirit, suddenly these words burst from my lips:

"Purge my ministry! Holy Spirit, please purge my ministry!"

Purge my ministry? I had no idea what The Holy Spirit was trying to communicate to the Father. But, I trusted Him. Within 7 days or so, someone that I really trusted in my ministry was caught in a terrible and tragic sin. It had been going on periodically for some time. I was too focused to notice their erratic behavior. But, The Holy Spirit protected me. He was praying through me to the Father that anything unlike Him would be stripped away from our work for God.

Millions have never tapped into this supernatural power. Yet, those who are moving toward a life of total addiction to The Holy Spirit, are tasting the most uncommon events of their lifetime.

► You have not been *everywhere*...yet everywhere continues to exist without your experiencing it.

► You do not know *everybody*...yet everybody continues to live each day quite well without knowing you.

► Likewise, you do not know *every* operation of The Holy Spirit, yet millions continue to taste the supernatural and uncommon events in their communication with Him...whether you will ever discover Him or not.

9 Helpful Keys In Developing Your Prayer Language

1.   **Acknowledge That You Do Not Know How To Pray Effectively Through Your Own Logic And Mind.**

2.   **Recognize That Many Times You Do Not Really Know What To Pray About, So It Is Important To Permit The Holy Spirit To Pray Through You.**

3.   **Recognize The Holy Spirit As Your Earthly Intercessor And Jesus As Your Heavenly Intercessor.** Permit them to work through your life.

4.   **Trust The Holy Spirit.** He will not fail you nor lead you into error. Remember, He is the Spirit of truth. (Read John 16:13.)

5. Ask For The Prayer Language. "...ye have not, because ye ask not," (James 4:2). Anything you ask in His name, you will receive it according to His will.

6. Be Willing To Grow Into The Experience. It may not happen immediately or overnight. Step by step, line upon line, you can begin to build your relationship with The Holy Spirit.

7. Ask The Holy Spirit To Draw You Toward Him. This is the greatest and most important prayer you could ever pray in your whole lifetime. *When you get in His presence, you will change.*

8. Recognize And Treasure Every Mentor That Provides More Revelation About Him.

9. Walk In The Present Light You Have And More Will Be Provided.

Our Prayer Together...
"Precious Holy Spirit, You gave the whole earth languages to communicate, connect and strengthen relationships. Animals have sounds. Humans have words. Holy Spirit, You have a special prayer language for me. Teach me, step by step, how to enter into the supernatural prayer life. You are my Intercessor on earth. I celebrate and value each moment in Your presence today. I am willing to make new discoveries. I will pursue You because You are The Spirit of truth. In Jesus' name. Amen."

❧ 9 ❧

THE HOLY SPIRIT IS THE SOURCE OF THE ANOINTING FOR YOUR LIFE

The Anointing Is The Power of God.

It *removes* burdens. It *destroys* yokes that enemies place upon you. The anointing stops any progress of your enemy *immediately.*

I have heard several ministers define the anointing as the "burden-removing, yoke-destroying power of God." I think that explains it wonderfully. "And it shall come to pass in that day, that His burden shall be taken away from off thy shoulder, and His yoke from off thy neck, and the yoke shall be destroyed because of the anointing," (Isaiah 10:27).

17 Facts You Should Know About The Anointing

1. The Anointing of The Holy Spirit Upon Jesus Enabled Him To Heal The Sick And Cast Out Devils. "How God anointed Jesus of Nazareth with the Holy Ghost and with power: who went about doing good, and healing all that were oppressed of the devil; for God was with Him," (Acts 10:38).

2. The Anointing Creates Fear In The Heart of Demonic Spirits. They are subject to that anointing, the power of God. When that anointing begins to flow and be released through you, any plan satan concocted is immediately sabotaged and destroyed. Satan does not fear you, but, rather that anointing which flows through you. That power is the fragrance of The Holy Spirit within you. "And when He was come to the other side into the country of the Gergesenes, there met Him two possessed with devils, coming out of the tombs, exceeding fierce, so that no man might pass by that way. And, behold, they cried out saying, What have we to do with Thee, Jesus, thou Son of God? art Thou come hither to torment us before the time?" (Matthew 8:28-29).

3. Jesus Knew That The Anointing of The Spirit Would Enable His Disciples To Stand Against Anything. "But ye shall receive power, after that the Holy Ghost is come upon you: and ye shall be witnesses unto Me both in Jerusalem, and in all Judaea, and in Samaria, and unto the uttermost part of the earth," (Acts 1:8).

That is why Jesus was devastated when Peter denied Him 3 times. When the disciples fled at the crucifixion, Jesus was not hopeless. He knew The Holy Spirit. He knew what the anointing would do within a person's life. His instruction was to tarry in the Upper Room until The Holy Spirit came. Jesus was not merely trying to make the disciples strong. He was trying to make them *aware* of The Holy Spirit.

4. The Anointing Is Not Necessarily Energy And Enthusiasm. It is not motion. It is not excitement. It is not noise. It is not mere exuberance and emotional strength.

5. The Anointing Is The Power of God To Handle Any Enemy Present In Your Life. "Not that we are sufficient of ourselves to think any thing as of ourselves; but our sufficiency is of God," (2 Corinthians 3:5).

6. The Holy Spirit Imparts A Specific Anointing Which Abides With You. "But the anointing which ye have received of Him abideth in you," (1 John 2:27).

7. The Holy Spirit Also Imparts Specific Anointings At Particular Moments of Need. I have seen it in healing crusades. Suddenly, like a wind, The Holy Spirit moves across an auditorium and eyes suddenly open, ears are unstopped, cancers disappear and the crippled leap from wheel chairs. That specific anointing is released through the *unity of faith* in that congregation. *Expectation is the mountain that crushes the pebble called satan.* When an entire audience can concentrate their faith and focus on Jesus, the power of The Holy Spirit is released in that place against sickness, disease and pain. Hundreds of miracles can happen simultaneously when the anointing is released through *agreement and unity.* "Behold, how good and how pleasant it is for brethren to dwell in unity!" (Psalm 133:1).

8. It Is Dangerous To Criticize Those Who Carry The Anointing of The Holy Spirit. "Touch not Mine anointed, and do My prophets no harm," (Psalm 105:15). It is a dangerous thing to treat lightly that supernatural anointing. You see, The Holy Spirit chooses the person He anoints. Men do not choose that anointing. Crowds cannot decide who carries that anointing.

9. The Holy Spirit Selects His Anointed. "The Spirit of the Lord God is upon me; because the

Lord hath anointed me to preach good tidings unto the meek; He hath sent me to bind up the brokenhearted, to proclaim liberty to the captives, and the opening of the prison to them that are bound," (Isaiah 61:1).

10. The Anointing You Respect Is The Anointing That Grows In Your Life. When you respect the anointing for healing, the miracles of healing begin to flow. When you respect an anointing for financial breakthrough, chains will fall off your life. Ideas and favor will flow like currents, mighty and unstoppable. When you treasure the anointing for revelation, knowledge will explode within you like a volcano. "...whatsoever ye shall ask in prayer, believing, ye shall receive," (Matthew 21:22).

11. When You Respect Those Who Are Anointed, Access Will Be Given To Them. The anointing occurred in different ways throughout the Bible. In the Old Testament, the anointing came as The Holy Spirit visited men such as Saul. When he would get in the presence of other prophets, he would begin to prophecy *under that anointing.* (Read 1 Samuel 9-10.)

12. The Anointing Upon You Is For Ministry To Others. Jesus felt this when He told His disciples that somebody had touched Him. He described it as "virtue has left my body." When His disciples said that many people had been touching Him, He simply said *it—somebody touched Me with a purpose in mind. Something has been emptied from Me.*

That is the purpose of the anointing—the power of God is in you to deliver those in captivity, and break down prison doors. "The Spirit of the Lord God is upon me; because the Lord hath anointed me to preach good tidings unto the meek; He hath sent me to bind up the broken hearted, to proclaim liberty to the captives, and the opening of the prison to them that are bound...to comfort all that mourn...to give unto them beauty for ashes, the oil of joy for mourning, the garment of praise for the spirit of heaviness," (Isaiah 61:1-3).

13. You Can Walk In The Anointing Every Moment of Your Life. As you yield to the leadership of The Holy Spirit, you can begin to live under that anointing. The Spirit of God is the Source of that power. He *qualifies* you. He *schedules* you. He *assigns* you. He turns you into a deliverer, instead of a captive. The disciples knew this. "Go ye into all the world, and preach the gospel," (Mark 16:15).

14. That Anointing Must Be Protected. You see, it is not a frivolous thing to carry the glory and the presence of God around in your life. It is a holy thing. You will be held responsible for guarding and nurturing it. "But foolish and unlearned questions avoid," (2 Timothy 2:23).

15. There Are Special Times That An Uncommon Anointing Is Placed Upon You For A Specific Reason. After a church service one night, the pastor met me in his office with tears in his eyes. "My brother, you don't really know how God used you tonight," he cried. As he shared with me private and confidential situations existing in his church, I realized that The Holy Spirit had given me words very uncommon that night for a reason. This man of God needed an uncommon demonstration of the care and compassion of God. He needed a turnaround. So, The Holy Spirit placed an unusual mantle on me for that service, to *solve that specific problem* in that specific church. Heaven came down and chains were broken that night.

16. Ask The Holy Spirit To Anoint You For The Work He Has Called You To Do. "Ask, and it shall be given you; seek, and you shall find; knock, and it shall be opened unto you: For everyone that asketh receiveth; and he that seeketh findeth; and to him that knocketh it shall be opened," (Matthew 7:7-8).

17. Treasure Every Moment The Holy Spirit Does Something Specific And Unique Through You. Don't laugh it off. Do not tease about it. And, do not elaborate and discuss it at length with the wrong people. Humbly thank Him for the privilege of being used to bring healing to the broken.

Our Prayer Together...
"Heavenly Father, thank You for The Holy Spirit. Thank You for the anointing, the burden-removing and yoke-destroying power of God. I need Your anointing. I respect those to whom You have given Your anointing. I will not criticize any man or woman of God who carries Your presence, Your voice, Your truths or Your power. What I respect will come toward me. So, I ask You today to send every good and perfect gift that You want me to have. Because I have honored You, obeyed and received Your instructions, I know Your anointing will flow through me today. In Jesus' name. Amen."

❧ **10** ❧

THE HOLY SPIRIT LOVES TO TALK TO YOU ABOUT EVERYTHING

━━━━━━▶❂◀━━━━━━

The Holy Spirit Loves Conversation.

30 Facts You Should Know About The Holy Spirit Talking To You

1.   The Holy Spirit Is A Communicator. When He comes, your speech changes immediately. "And it shall come to pass afterward, that I will pour out My spirit upon all flesh; and your sons and your daughters shall prophesy," (Joel 2:28). (See also Acts 2:16-18.)

2.   The Holy Spirit Affected The Words of Thousands On The Day of Pentecost. "And there appeared unto them cloven tongues like as of fire, and it sat upon each of them. And they were all filled with the Holy Ghost, and began to speak with other tongues, as the Spirit gave them utterance," (Acts 2:3-4).

3.   The Holy Spirit Was Involved When Jesus Gave Commandments To The Apostles Before His Ascension. "Until the day in which He was taken up, after that He through the Holy Ghost had given commandments unto the apostles whom He had chosen," (Acts 1:2).

4.   The Holy Spirit Influences Your Conversations With Others. "But ye shall receive power, after that the Holy Ghost is come upon you: and ye shall be witnesses unto Me both in Jerusalem, and in all Judaea, and in Samaria, and unto the uttermost part of the earth," (Acts 1:8).

5.   The Holy Spirit Affects The Boldness And Aggressiveness of Your Conversations With Others. "And when they had prayed, the place was shaken where they were assembled together; and they were all filled with the Holy Ghost, and they spake the word of God with boldness," (Acts 4:31).

6.   The First Proof And Evidence of The Holy Spirit In Your Life Is The Change In Your Conversation. It was obvious in the life of Peter. He was weak and intimidated by others before Pentecost. *Afterwards,* he was bold and specific: "Then Peter, filled with the Holy Ghost, said unto them...Be it known unto you all, and to all the people of Israel, that by the name of Jesus Christ of Nazareth, whom ye crucified, whom God raised from the dead, even by Him doth this man stand here before you whole...Neither is there salvation in any other: for there is none other name under Heaven given among men, whereby we must be saved. Now when they saw the boldness of Peter and John, and perceived that they were unlearned and ignorant men, they marvelled; and they took knowledge of them, that they had been with Jesus," (Acts 4:8, 10, 12-13).

7.   The Holy Spirit Talks More Than Any Other Person On Earth. "He that hath an ear, let him hear what the Spirit saith unto the churches," (Revelation 2:7, 11, 17 and Revelation 3:6, 13, 22).

8.   The Holy Spirit Expects You To Continu-

ously Listen For His Voice. "The hearing ear, and the seeing eye, the Lord hath made even both of them," (Proverbs 20:12).

9.   The Holy Spirit Will Teach You. "He shall teach you all things," (John 14:26).

10.   The Holy Spirit Will Remind You of The Principles of Jesus. "...and bring all things to your remembrance, whatsoever I have said unto you," (John 14:26).

11.   The Holy Spirit Will Talk To You About Sin In Your Life. "And when He is come, He will reprove the world of sin, and of righteousness, and of judgment," (John 16:8). "Come now, and let us reason together, saith the Lord: though your sins be as scarlet, they shall be as white as snow; though they be red like crimson, they shall be as wool," (Isaiah 1:18).

12.   The Holy Spirit Will Talk To You About Things In Your Future. "He will shew you things to come," (John 16:13).

13.   The Holy Spirit Will Talk To You About Those To Whom You Are Assigned. "Then the Spirit said unto Philip, Go near, and join thyself to this chariot," (Acts 8:29).

14.   The Holy Spirit Will Talk To You About The Motives of Others Around You. "And the Spirit bade me go with them, nothing doubting," (Acts 11:12).

15.   The Holy Spirit Will Talk To You About Your Specific Assignment. "As they ministered to the Lord, and fasted, the Holy Ghost said, Separate me Barnabas and Saul for the work whereunto I have called them," (Acts 13:2).

16.   The Holy Spirit Will Discuss The Location And Geographical Area of Your

Assignment. "So they, being sent forth by the Holy Ghost, departed unto Seleucia; and from thence they sailed to Cyprus," (Acts 13:4).

17. The Holy Spirit Will Reveal Those On Whom Judgment Is Coming And Falling. "Then Saul, (who also is called Paul,) filled with the Holy Ghost, set his eyes on him, And said, O full of all subtlety and all mischief, thou child of the devil, thou enemy of all righteousness, wilt thou not cease to pervert the right ways of the Lord," (Acts 13:9-10).

18. The Holy Spirit Will Talk To You About Things That Are Essential And Nonessential. "For it seemed good to the Holy Ghost, and to us, to lay upon you no greater burden than these necessary things," (Acts 15:28).

19. The Holy Spirit Will Talk To You About The Place of Provision And Supply. "Get thee hence, and turn thee eastward, and hide thyself by the brook...I have commanded the ravens to feed thee there," (1 Kings 17:3-4). This is evident here in the life of Elijah.

20. The Holy Spirit Will Talk To You About Other People. Your attitude. Trivia. The Secret Place. Samuel experienced this as a lad. God talked to him about Eli, his spiritual mentor. (See 1 Samuel 3:1.)

That is why it is important for you to have a special place to meet with Him every day. I call my private place of prayer, The Secret Place.

21. You Must Move Away From The Voices of Others When You Really Want To Hear The Voice of The Holy Spirit.

▶ Solitude is necessary for intimacy.

▶ Intimacy is necessary for impartation.

▶ Impartation is necessary for change.

You can only change when The Holy Spirit is speaking into your life. Now, The Holy Spirit speaks to us in various ways.

22. The Words of The Holy Spirit Energize And Bring Life. "It is the Spirit that quickeneth; the flesh profiteth nothing: the words that I speak unto you, they are spirit, and they are life," (John 6:63).

Thank God for your pastor, the gift from The Holy Spirit to your life. He warns you. Comforts you. Strengthens you. Develop the discipline of church attendance—even when the busyness of your life overwhelms you. When you are exposed to the preaching of a man of God, the chances of your success are multiplied over and over.

23. The Holy Spirit Will Talk To You About Coming Into His Presence. "Come ye, and let us go up to the mountain of the Lord, to the house of the God of Jacob; and He will teach us of His ways, and we will walk in His paths: for out of Zion shall go forth the law, and the word of the Lord from Jerusalem," (Isaiah 2:3).

24. The Holy Spirit Will Talk To You About Accountability. "So then every one of us should give account of himself to God," (Romans 14:12).

25. The Holy Spirit Talks To Children. "Children, obey your parents in the Lord: for this is right. Honor thy father and mother; (which is the first commandment with promise;) That it may be well with thee, and thou mayest live long on the earth," (Ephesians 6:1-3).

26. The Holy Spirit Talks To Husbands. "Husbands, love your wives, even as Christ also loved the church, and gave Himself for it...So ought men to love their wives as their own bodies," (Ephesians 5:25, 28).

27. The Holy Spirit Talks To Wives. "Wives, submit yourselves unto your own husbands, as unto the Lord," (Ephesians 5:22).

28. The Holy Spirit Will Talk To The Father About You. "Likewise the Spirit also helpeth our infirmities: for we know not what we should pray for as we ought: but the Spirit itself maketh intercession for us with groanings which cannot be uttered. And He that searcheth the hearts knoweth what is the mind of the Spirit, because He maketh intercession for the saints according to the will of God," (Romans 8:26-27).

29. The Holy Spirit Will Talk To You And Confirm That You Belong To God. "The Spirit itself beareth witness with our spirit, that we are the children of God," (Romans 8:16).

30. The Holy Spirit Will Talk To You About Sowing A Significant Seed During A Time of Crisis In Your Life. It happened to me in a crusade in Kansas. A tall young man sat on the front seat. He would shake his head every time I said something about financial prosperity. It agitated me. But, I kept speaking and sharing the Word of the Lord. Suddenly, The Holy Spirit spoke to my heart. "Empty your entire wallet to him after the service tonight." I was sickened inside. You see, I had just cashed a large check. In fact, I had 9 $100 bills and another $200 for a total of $1100. I had plans and needs. Yet, The Holy Spirit nudged me to empty my entire wallet.

I replied, "If you will remind me after church, I will do it." Something within me was hoping he would leave! I really had no desire whatsoever to give someone like this *anything!*

After the service, he walked up to me and started a conversation. I said, "The Holy Spirit told me to empty my wallet into you." I handed him $1100 cash. He looked at it, and kept talking. He shoved it in his pocket and never said a word.

I became upset. When I returned to the hotel, I complained strongly to God. "I just gave him $1100. He never even spoke a thank you!"

"Why did you do it?"

"Well, You told me to do it!" was my reply.

He indicated that I was to simply *shut up!* The next day, a phone call came to me worth a minimum of $25,000 to my future. You see, when The Holy Spirit talks to you about a Seed, *He has a Harvest on His mind.*

It happened to the widow of Zarephath. The man of God came to her and talked to her about sowing Seed. It was not his idea at all. The Holy Spirit had instructed him while sitting by the brook, Cherith. He obeyed *God.* The widow obeyed *him.* And, the supply continued throughout the days of the famine.

▶ When The Holy Spirit talks, *obey.*
▶ When The Holy Spirit speaks to you, *changes are beginning.*
▶ When The Holy Spirit talks, *joy will flood your heart.*

"While it is said, To day if ye will hear his voice, harden not your hearts, as in the day of provocation," (Hebrews 3:15).

3 Ways The Holy Spirit Will Talk To You

1.   The Holy Spirit Speaks To You Through Men of God. These wonderful men of God inspire our faith and correct our focus. When you obey the instructions of The Holy Spirit through a man of God, you will prosper beyond your imagination. "Believe in the Lord your God, so shall ye be established; believe His prophets, so shall ye prosper," (2 Chronicles 20:20).

2.   The Holy Spirit Speaks Through Your Conscience. When Stephen, full of faith and power, did great wonders and miracles among the people, some disputed with him. Their *conscience* reacted. "And they were not able to resist the Wisdom and the spirit by which he spake," (Acts 6:10). They became so angry, they rose up and stoned this great man of God. The Holy Spirit used their own conscience to convict them.

3.   The Holy Spirit Speaks To You Through The Scriptures. He moved on men of old to document these holy Words of God to us. Picture every Word like a Seed. Within each Word is an invisible and powerful fragrance called joy. Uncommon joy is the hidden essence of each Word of God. When you hear His Words and embrace them, you are receiving Holy Seed into the soil of your life. An explosion of unexplainable joy will come forth out of those Seeds like an energizing fragrance. I cannot explain it. It happens every day of my life. The moment I read His Words, changes begin within me.

Our Prayer Together...
"Holy Spirit, thank You for being the wonderful

gift as my Companion. You are my Mentor, my Teacher, and treasured Friend. Thank You for taking the time to talk to me, converse with me, and reveal instructions to me. Forgive me for the times I have not listened, obeyed and completed Your Word. If I have failed to complete any instruction, please speak again to me in such a way I cannot doubt it. Unclutter my life of distractions so that I may hear Your voice and obey You without question. In Jesus' name. Amen."

❧ 1 Corinthians 7:20 ❧

"Let every man abide in the same calling
wherein he was called."

Section 2

THE ASSIGNMENT

∾ Psalm 139:3 ∾

"Thou compassest my path and my
lying down, and art acquainted
with all my ways."

∼ **11** ∼

EVERYTHING GOD CREATED WAS CREATED TO SOLVE A PROBLEM

You Were Created To Solve A Problem.

Creativity is the search for solutions. In large gatherings, speakers could not be heard clearly. So, the microphone and public address system were created. Eyeglasses were created for those who have difficulty in seeing.

Problems are the catalyst for creativity. When an inventor—whether it is Thomas Edison, or whomever—invents something, their creativity is based on an existing problem. They *solve* the problem, and they are *rewarded* accordingly.

Why did you buy your car? It solved a *transportation* problem.

Why do you watch the news each evening on television? It solves an *information* problem.

Mechanics solve *car* problems.

Dentists solve *teeth* problems.

Lawyers solve *legal* problems.

Mothers solve *emotional* problems.

Accountants solve *tax* problems.

That is why God created us. God wanted a *love* relationship. He wanted to be chosen, pursued and *treasured*.

Now Adam had a problem; he needed *human* companionship. "And the Lord God said, It is not good that the man should be alone; I will make him an help meet for him...And the Lord God caused a deep sleep to fall upon Adam, and he slept: and He took one of his ribs, and closed up the flesh instead thereof; And the rib, which the Lord God had taken from man, made He a woman, and brought her unto the man. And Adam said, This is now bone of my bones, and flesh of my flesh: she shall be called Woman, because she was taken out of Man," (Genesis 2:18, 21-23).

You see, each one of us is a *solution*.

So when you open your eyes every morning, you are looking into an entire world crowned with solutions. Everything created is a solution...to somebody, somewhere, at some time.

You are a walking solution to somebody.

This means you are a reward to someone. Somebody *needs* you. Somebody *wants* you. You are *necessary* to somebody, somewhere...*today*.

Read these powerful words. "Then the word of the Lord came unto me, saying, Before I formed thee in the belly I knew thee; and before thou camest forth out of the womb I sanctified thee, and I ordained thee a prophet unto the nations," (Jeremiah 1:4-5).

God is not a respecter of persons. He created Jeremiah for a special time, season and for a special people. It is the same with you.

You were created for a specific and very special purpose...*to solve a specific problem on earth.* I call this, *The Assignment.*

"I am fearfully and wonderfully made: marvellous are Thy works; and that my soul knoweth right well. My substance was not hid from Thee, when I was made in secret, and curiously wrought in the lowest parts of the earth. Thine eyes did see my substance, yet being unperfect; and in Thy book all my members were written, which in continuance were fashioned, when as yet there was none of them," (Psalm 139:14-16).

8 Important Facts About Your Assignment

1. God Is Totally Focused On You, Your Ways And Your Assignment. "Thou compassest my path and my lying down, and art acquainted with all my ways," (Psalm 139:3).

2. God Carefully Examines Every Word You Speak Daily. "For there is not a word in my tongue, but, lo, O Lord, Thou knowest it altogether," (Psalm 139:4).

3. The Holy Spirit, Who Created You, Is With You Continuously. He keeps His hand upon your life. "Thou hast beset me behind and before, and laid Thine hand upon me," (Psalm 139:5).

4. You Will Never Be Outside of His Reach or Access. "Whither shall I go from Thy Spirit? or whither shall I flee from Thy presence? If I ascend up into Heaven, Thou art there: if I make my bed in hell, behold, Thou art there. If I take the wings of the morning, and dwell in the uttermost parts of the sea; even there shall Thy hand lead me, and Thy right hand shall hold me," (Psalm 139:7-10).

5. When You Are In The Darkest Trial of Your Life, He Will Turn On The Light For You To Enable You To Complete This Assignment He Planted Within You. "If I say, Surely the darkness shall cover me; even the night shall be light about me. Yea, the darkness hideth not from Thee; but the night shineth as the day: the darkness and the light are both alike to Thee. For Thou hast possessed my reins: Thou has covered me in my mother's womb," (Psalm 139:11-13).

6. **It Is Impossible To Count The Pleasurable Thoughts That Pour Out From The Mind of God Towards You Daily.** "How precious also are Thy thoughts unto me, O God! how great is the sum of them! If I should count them, they are more in number than the sand: when I awake. I am still with thee," (Psalm 139:17-18).

7. **It Is Your Own Responsibility To Identify Your Assignment.** So, do not expect others to define your Assignment for you. It is not their responsibility to do so. *They have a personal responsibility to discover their own Assignment.* You must discover your own Assignment for yourself. God intended it to be so. This will require your personal reaching, pursuing and moving *toward His presence.* "So then every one of us shall give account of himself to God," (Romans 14:12).

8. **The Word of God Is The Blueprint For Your Assignment And Must Become Your Daily Focus.** Hearing from Him will make your Assignment clear, irrefutable and immovable. "Thou hast dealt well with Thy servant, O Lord, according unto Thy word," (Psalm 119:65).

You are on earth to solve a problem.
That is why it is called...The Assignment.

❧ **12** ❧

YOU ARE A REWARD TO SOMEONE

———————◆═◆═◆═———————

Somebody Needs You.

Moses was needed as a leader to the children of Israel. He was their *reward.*

David was needed by the Israelites to defeat Goliath. He was a *reward* to King Saul as well, when he defeated Goliath and routed the Philistines.

Naomi needed a caretaker. Ruth was a reward for her. Her devotion was recorded in the Scriptures for people to read about throughout many generations.

The Jews would have been destroyed except for Esther. Esther was their answer, their solution, their *reward.*

Pharaoh desperately needed someone to interpret his dream. Joseph was a reward to him and subsequently to the people of Egypt.

Famine would have destroyed the Egyptians. Joseph was *their* reward because he interpreted the message from God through the dream of Pharaoh.

You see, every person God created is a *reward* to somebody.

Think about this. It is very important that you grasp *your* significance and value.

Your *patience* is a reward for somebody that others would not tolerate. Your *words* will motivate someone incapable of seeing what you see. It may be the mental, emotional or spiritual qualities God has developed within you. *But somebody desperately needs you today.*

God planned you. Nobody else can be like you. *Nobody else* can do what you do. You are unlike anyone else on earth. Grasp this. Embrace it. God is not a duplicator. He is a Creator. You are absolutely perfect and genetically accurate for *solving a specific problem* for somebody on earth.

Somebody needs exactly what you have been given by God. Somebody is hungry and thirsty for *your* presence. Somebody will starve *without you* entering their life. Someone is literally dying emotionally, mentally or spiritually, *waiting for you* to come along and rescue them. Somebody has been lying awake at night praying that God would send you into their life.

You are their reward.

Now, it is important that you recognize that some people do not really need you. You are *not* their answer. You are *not* their solution. Do not take offense at this. God has somebody else planned for them.

You are not needed *everywhere.* You are only needed at a specific *place,* at a specific *time* and for a specific *person.*

Now, this person (or people) has *qualified* for your entrance into their life. They may not initially see you as being their reward, but you really are. You are *exactly* what God has ordered for their life.

Meditate on this truth. *Taste* it. *Feel* it.

5 Important Keys To Remember

1. God Has Qualified You To Be A Perfect Solution To Someone.

2. It Is The Responsibility of Others To Discern Your Assignment To Them. The Pharisees did not discern that Jesus was assigned to them. But Zacchaeus did, and a relationship was born. Even Pharaoh of Egypt, an unbeliever, discerned that Joseph was the answer to his dream and dilemma. Thousands were sick and blind, but, one cried out, "Jesus, Thou son of David, have mercy on me," (see Mark 10:47).

3. When You Discover To Whom You Have Been Assigned, You Will Experience Great Peace, Fulfillment And Provision For Your Own Life. You must determine and know well the anointing and calling on your own life. Stand strong, and stay linked to The Holy Spirit in total dependency, and God will direct you.

4. You Must Look For Opportunities To Heal, Strengthen And Bless Others. Do good every time it is possible. "Withhold not good from them to whom it is due, when it is in the power of thine hand to do it," (Proverbs 3:27).

5. Your Assignment Will Always Be To Someone With A Problem. *Someone close to you is hurting.* John, the beloved disciple, urged compassion. "But whoso hath this world's good, and seeth his brother have need, and shutteth up his bowels of compassion from him, how dwelleth the love of God in him?" (1 John 3:17).

15 Principles In Problem-Solving You Must Recognize And Apply When Helping Others

1. Someone Needs You. *Someone with a problem.* Somebody with a health problem needs a doctor. Somebody with an automobile problem needs a mechanic. Somebody with a financial problem needs a banker. Somebody with a spiritual problem needs a minister.

You see, problems are really wonderful things. They make us reach for each other. They enable us to see the value of those close to us. They enable others to observe our importance as well. So never run from a problem. Simply run toward the solution.

2.   Some Problems Will Be More Noticeable Than Others.   Tailors notice missing buttons. Mechanics hear something wrong in car engines. Why? That is their specific Assignment.

3.   God Expects You To Move Swiftly To Solve A Problem For Those To Whom You Are Assigned. "Withhold not good from them to whom it is due, when it is in the power of thine hand to do it," (Proverbs 3:27).

4.   Your Assignment Will Determine And Heighten What You See And Hear. You will see things others close to you do not notice. You will *hear* things in a conversation that others may overlook. The problem you *notice* is a clue to your anointing and calling in life.

5.   You Are Not Assigned To Everybody With A Problem. Some problems are impossible for you to solve. Somebody else has been assigned to solve those *specific problems* for people. However, you must learn to stay in the *center of your expertise*, the solutions you contain.

6.   The Holy Spirit Will Answer Every Important Question You Ask. His answers will bring great peace to your heart. "Call unto Me, and I will answer thee, and show thee great and mighty things, which thou knowest not," (Jeremiah 33:3). Ask Him honestly if the problem you are seeing is the penalty for an act of disobedience or rebellion. Why? *Never breathe life into something God is killing.* The last thing you want to do is to oppose the workings of God in the life of someone.

Let me explain. Recently, someone was discussing their son with me. She said, "I feel so sorry for him. He has been out of work for several months. So, I have been giving him spending money and letting him stay at the house. Could you help him in some way?"

Further discussion revealed that the young man was unbelievably lazy. He had presented no resumes at any companies. He had *refused* to do small chores around the church. He had not even mowed the grass at his mother's home, nor washed and waxed her car during the days he was "out of work."

I encouraged her to *withdraw* her support. I explained that in Deuteronomy 28 God said He would only bless "the work of our hands." Paul wrote to the church at Thessalonica, "For even when we were with you, this we commanded you, that if any would not work, neither should he eat. For we hear that there are some which walk among you disorderly, *working not at all,*" (2 Thessalonians 3:10-11).

The Bible says to withdraw yourself from lazy people. Part from them. "And if any man obey not our word by this epistle, note that man, and have no company with him, that he may be ashamed," (2 Thessalonians 3:14).

Now, he is *not* an enemy. He is a *brother.* But he must be taught the *law of productivity,* that increase involves work.

Ask The Holy Spirit, "Is this person having a problem due to ignorance? Am I assigned to teach them?" You see, this is what Philip did when he ran to the Ethiopian eunuch and asked, "Understandest thou what thou readest?" (Acts 8:30). Now, the eunuch was not learned, but he wanted to be taught! Philip did not have to force him to become a student. "And he said, How can I, except some man should guide me? And he desired Philip that he would come up and sit with him," (Acts 8:31).

Ask The Holy Spirit, "Am I the one that you've assigned to solve this problem for this person?" If you are, great joy will enter you as you bond and interact with this person for a solution to their problem. This is why the Scripture emphasizes in Proverbs 3:27, "Withhold not good from them to whom it is due, when it is in the power of thine hand to do it."

Ask The Holy Spirit, "Have you qualified me to solve this problem and is this the right time to do so?" You see, the Scriptures instruct us to solve a problem "...when it is in the power of thine hand to do it," (Proverbs 3:27).

I often see many problems I *want* to solve. But The Holy Spirit *forbids* me. I do not always know why. But, He has a specific plan. Paul experienced this also. "Now when they had gone throughout Phrygia and the region of Galatia, and were forbidded of the Holy Ghost to preach the word in Asia, After they were come to Mysia, they assayed to go into Bithynia: but the Spirit suffered them not," (Acts 16:6-7).

7. Accept That The Holy Spirit Will Forbid You To Solve Problems For Some People. Now, it would seem to anyone that the gospel preached by Paul would solve a problem for everybody anywhere he went. But, God always has a plan.

He has *reasons*.

He has *seasons*.

"To every thing there is a season, and a time to every purpose under the Heaven: A time to be born, and a time to die; a time to plant, and a time to pluck up that which is planted; A time to kill, and a time to heal; a time to break down, and a time to build up," (Ecclesiastes 3:1-3).

8.   Stay Aware That The Attitude of The Person With The Problem Is More Important To God Than The Problem They Are Facing. You see, a rebel is not in position to receive from the Lord. But, "If ye be willing and obedient, ye shall eat the good of the land," (Isaiah 1:19).

Timing is so vital to The Holy Spirit. Permit Him to direct your steps in this area *every single day* of your life. "Behold, I stand at the door, and knock; if any man hear My voice, and open the door, I will come in to him, and will sup with him, and he with Me," (Revelation 3:20).

9.   God Will Give You Great Compassion For The Person With The Problem.

10.   God Will Provide You With Understanding And Time To Respond Properly To The Problem.

11.   The Person Will Have Great Confidence In Your Ability And Calling To Solve The Problem For Them. (See Acts 8:31-39 and Genesis 41:37-42.)

12.   God Will Confirm Your Assignment With Inner Peace In You And With Joy In Them. (See Genesis 41:15-44.)

13.   It Will Always Be At A Critical Turning

Point In That Person's Life.

14. It Will Never Take You Away From Your Time With The Holy Spirit And Private Prayer. "But seek ye first the kingdom of God, and His righteousness; and all these things shall be added unto you," (Matthew 6:33).

Emergencies that take you out of His presence, out of your time spent with God, are usually orchestrated by hell *to break the rhythm of your spiritual life.*

Every pastor recalls "emergency phone calls" that came just before his preaching service. It was intended to *break his focus*, dilute his enthusiasm and derail the service.

15. If It Is The Will of God For You To Solve A Problem For Someone, You Will Have The Ability And The Provision To Do So. "Withhold not good from them to whom it is due, *when it is in the power of thine hand to do it*," (Proverbs 3:27).

A couple approached me recently at one of my Schools of The Holy Spirit. They were congenial, warm and very loving. He spoke, "Did you receive my phone call?"

"Yes, I did," I replied.

"I called you over 10 times, but you never returned my telephone calls."

"My secretary told you that I *require an explanation* of the phone call before I return any telephone calls," I explained carefully. "You see, I receive thousands of telephone calls because I have a television and radio ministry as well. I have established guidelines. If you do not respect my secretary enough to follow my instructions through her, *you are disqualified for a return telephone call.*"

The young man then said, "The Holy Spirit told my wife and I that you were going to give us $10,000."

"Well, that was not The Holy Spirit who told you that. Two reasons: First, I do not know you at all, and it is written, '...we beseech you, brethren, *to know them* which labour among you, and are over you in the Lord,' (1 Thessalonians 5:12). I have not met you. I am unaware of the mentorship and the authority over your life. The second reason is very obvious: I do not have $10,000 to give you. The Holy Spirit would never tell me to give something I do not even possess."

They were crestfallen. But I was not assigned to give them $10,000.

Of course, I prayed with them that the Lord would carefully guide their affairs and direct them to the necessary relationships and provision.

▶ You are not assigned to *everybody*.

▶ You are not assigned *everywhere*.

▶ You cannot solve *every kind* of problem.

Refuse to be manipulated, dominated or intimidated by the unreasonable demands and expectations of others. When God is involved, your Assignment will always be to someone with a problem God has qualified you to solve.

You are a reward from God to somebody. Never forget it.

RECOMMENDED INVESTMENTS:
Finding Your Purpose In Life (Book/B-05/32 pgs)
The Assignment Vol. 3: The Trials & The Triumphs
  (Book/B-97/160 pgs)
The Assignment Vol. 4: The Pain & The Passion
  (Book/B-98/144 pgs)
The School of Wisdom #6, The Twelve Priorities of Life
  (CD/CDS-54)

"What You Love The Most Is
A Clue To The Gift You Contain."
                                    -MIKE MURDOCK

❧ 13 ❧

WHAT YOU LOVE MOST IS A CLUE TO YOUR ASSIGNMENT

━━━━━⟫▪◉▪⟪━━━━━

Passion Is Magnetic.

What do you love to *discuss?* What do you love to *hear about?* What *excites* you? These are clues to your Assignment. These are clues to your abilities. *You will always have a Wisdom toward whatever you love.*

If you love children, you will probably possess an innate and obvious Wisdom toward *children.*

If you love computers, you will discover a natural inclination to understand this *computer age.*

If you love to work on cars, you will have a natural Wisdom toward *mechanical things.*

Great singers do not normally say, "I really hate singing. I would rather sell cars. God is making me sing." Of course not. They *love* to sing.

You will never hear a great pianist say, "I hate playing the piano. It is something I *have* to do. God is *making* me do it. I would much rather be building houses."

You see, *what you love is a clue to your Assignment.*

When God calls you to an Assignment, obey Him. Within due time, He will birth an inner desire for that specific Assignment. It is one of the ways He honors your obedience.

Yet, some of us were taught the opposite. I remember one of the ladies in my father's church saying, "If God calls you to preach the gospel overseas and you refuse, He will *make* you go, just like He did with Jonah! If you tell God you do not want to do something, He will *make* you do it."

God gave Jonah an instruction to go to Nineveh. He chose to go to Tarshish. Note this. Why didn't he simply stay where he was? He did not have to leave where he was. *Something within him was moving him.* He simply refused to complete the Assignment.

His Assignment was two-fold: 1) leave where he was, and 2) arrive in Nineveh.

He *started* his Assignment. God dealt with him for his rebellion to complete his Assignment.

God is not looking for ways to antagonize you, agitate you and make you miserable. When He calls you to do something, if you will remain in His presence and stay obedient, He will give you a *desire to complete it*.

What *really* excites you?

What brings *great enthusiasm*?

What are you doing on the *happiest days* of your life?

Love births persistence. When you love something, you give birth to a tenacity, determination and persistence that is extraordinary. Recently, I read a powerful story about a runner. In his youth, he had a terrible disease. Doctors insisted he would never be able to even walk again. But, something powerful was within him. *He loved running.* His love for running birthed determination. He ended up winning a gold medal in the Olympics.

Love is stronger than sickness. It is stronger than disease. It is stronger than poverty. So, find what you truly and continuously love and *build your daily agenda around it.* I discussed this with my staff recently. If every human on earth was paid $10 an hour for work, regardless of the type of job, what would *you* do? For example, if you chose to be a janitor of a building, you would receive $10 an hour for it. A heart surgeon? You would still receive $10 an hour. What would you love to do if money were no longer a factor? *That is a clue to your life Assignment.*

Moses loved people. When he saw an Egyptian beating a fellow Israelite, he moved quickly. He was so passionate about justice that he killed the Egyptian. That was unfortunate. It postponed his Assignment. But his love for his people was a clue to his mantle as a deliverer. He was attentive to the *cries.* He *cared.* His compassion ran deep. Because he had a love for people, he was able to lead people. They followed him. Yes, they complained, whined and gripped, but they had found their leader.

Abraham loved peace. He despised conflict. So, when God decided to destroy Sodom and Gomorrah, Abraham became an intercessor and mediator for Lot, his nephew, who lived in Sodom and Gomorrah. His love for peace and justice was rewarded by God. Though Sodom and Gomorrah were destroyed, Lot and his daughters were brought out safely. It happened because Abraham contained something very precious, a love for peace. *His love for peace birthed the Wisdom necessary to achieve it.*

It is wise to alter and change the flaws within ourselves. It is even wiser to acknowledge and embrace the center of your calling.

Permit the *true you* to become strong. I have often

heard people insistently tell a shy person, "You must talk more!" Then, the same person will turn to someone talking a lot, "Be quiet! Just sit and listen!" We instruct youth, "Get more serious about life." We instruct the elderly, "You need to be less serious and lighten up!"

Do not move away from the essence of what God made you. Understand the importance of your *uniqueness*.

Discern your gifts. Name your calling. Build your daily agenda around it. Whatever you are gifted to do is what you should be doing.

What you truly love the most is a clue to a marvelous gift and quality inside you.

∾ 14 ∾

WHAT YOU HATE IS A CLUE TO SOMETHING YOU ARE ASSIGNED TO CORRECT

Anger Is Energy, Power And Ability.

However, it requires *proper focus.* Have you ever wondered why others were not angry about situations that infuriated you? Of course you have. This is a clue to your Assignment.

Remember These 3 Wisdom Keys

▶ *You Cannot Correct What You Are Unwilling To Confront.*

▶ *What You Permit Will Always Continue.*

▶ *Behavior Permitted Is Behavior Perpetuated.*

I have a love for Wisdom. I have a hatred of ignorance. In my own life I have attended seminars where Scriptures were misquoted, truth was distorted and error was dominant. It was almost impossible to sit and permit it.

You cannot really change or correct something unless you have a God-given hatred for it, whether it is sickness, injustice, racial prejudice, poverty, divorce or abortion.

Many things are wrong in this country. But, they will never be changed *until someone is angry enough* about it to step forward and take charge.

For instance, abortion has gradually become accepted, although it is a truly devastating blight on our conscience in this country. It appears that no articulate spokesperson has yet emerged who is capable of turning the tide, although I thank God for those who are making significant efforts to do so!

The persuaded are persuasive.

Often I have asked God to give us someone with a burning desire who can *successfully* plead the case of the unborn child. I have asked God to provide a militant, intellectual, passionate zealot who could link The Word of God with the gift of life in my generation— someone passionate and on fire.

That someone could be you.

I am not talking about the issue of bombing abortion clinics or murdering those who kill unborn children.

I am speaking of *an anointing,* a mantle and a calling—when someone *rises up* to complete their Assignment in this generation: to challenge, correct and conquer the Seeds of rebellion that have grown up around us.

Your anger is important. Do not ignore it. Satan dreads your fury. *An angry man is an awakened man.* An angry man changes the minds of others.

So pay attention to the things that ignite your anger, passion and strong feelings.

The Problem That Infuriates You The Most Is The Problem That God Has Assigned You To Solve.

Anger is a clue to your anointing and Assignment. When Moses saw an Egyptian beating an Israelite, anger rose up within him. That anger was a *clue.* It was a *signal*. The situation that infuriated him was the one God had ordained him to change, correct and alter. He was a deliverer.

Anger is the birthplace of change. Situations only change when anger is born. You will not solve a problem, consciously or unconsciously, until you experience a holy and righteous anger rising up within you.

You will not change a situation until it becomes intolerable.

For many years in the south, African Americans were forced by law to sit in the back of the bus. They might still be doing that today had it not been for a courageous woman, Rosa Parks. This work-weary black lady took her place on a crowded bus in Montgomery, Alabama. When the bus filled, she refused to stand for the white man to have her seat. It was the catalyst for dramatic, appropriate and long-needed change in America. That kind of courage deserves honor and respect.

Whatever You Can Tolerate, You Cannot Change. Whatever you refuse to accept, whatever makes you mad enough to take action, is a clue to your Assignment.

MADD, Mothers Against Drunk Driving, was started by a mother who saw her child killed on the street by a drunk driver. Her anger birthed a response.

If you can adapt to your present, you will never enter your future. Only those who cannot tolerate the present are qualified to enter their future.

It has happened in my own life. When I was a teenager, I felt a great attraction to the courtroom. I wanted to be an attorney. I sat for hours in those courtrooms in my little hometown of Lake Charles, Louisiana. I took notes by the hour on cases that came up. I still have a hatred of injustice. I can become angry about it right now while I am writing you this chapter just thinking about people who have not been represented properly. I read law books continually and still continuously read books dealing with the legal system. Watching the process of law and observing the manipulation that occurs in the courtroom, still infuriates me. I believe this *anger is a clue to the anointing on my life.*

Ignorance angers me. When I talk to people who are uninformed, something comes alive in me. The desire to teach is overwhelming. I speak at seminars throughout the world and sometimes almost miss my airplane schedule because I become so obsessed with teaching. Walking out of the seminar becomes extremely difficult.

Unproductive employees are a source of great agitation to me. I believe it is a clue to a mantle on my life. It is important to me that I unlock the mystery of achievement through Wisdom Keys and the books that I write.

Listen carefully to ministers who teach prosperity. *They hate poverty.* They despise lack. It grieves them deeply to see families wounded, destroyed and devastated because of poverty. Their messages are full of fury and sound almost angry! Why? Destroying poverty is a calling *within* them.

Have you ever listened to ministers with an anointing for deliverance? They become angry toward demonic spirits that possess family members.

Listen to a soul-winning evangelist. Hear his

passion? He is moved with compassion when he sees the unsaved and uncommitted come to Christ.

Anger reveals an anointing. "And it shall come to pass in that day, that His burden shall be taken away from off thy shoulder, and His yoke from off thy neck, and the yoke shall be destroyed *because of the anointing,*" (Isaiah 10:27). The anointing is the *burden-removing, yoke-destroying power of God in your life.*

So pay attention to whatever angers you. Something inside you rises up strong against it. Why? *Your anger qualifies you to be an enemy of that problem.* God is preparing you to solve it.

- ▶ Anger is *energy.*
- ▶ Anger is *power.*
- ▶ Anger *moves* hell.
- ▶ Anger can *master a situation.*

Unfocused anger destroys and ruins. Focused properly, it creates miraculous change. Anger merely requires proper focus. Develop it. You must see your anger as an instruction from God to stay in The Secret Place to *find the solution for the problem*, obtain the weapons to destroy the enemy, and *develop a daily agenda* designed by The Holy Spirit...to create change.

Angry people can dramatically change their generation.

⮥ 2 Corinthians 2:4 ⮥

"For out of much affliction and anguish of
heart I wrote unto you with many tears; not
that ye should be grieved, but that ye might
know the love which I have more
abundantly unto you."

≈ 15 ≈

WHAT GRIEVES YOU IS A CLUE TO SOMETHING YOU ARE ASSIGNED TO HEAL

Tears Talk.

What you cry about is a clue to something you were created and ordained by God to heal. *Compassion is a signpost.*

What grieves you? Battered wives? Abused and molested children? Ignorance? Disease? Poverty? Pornography? Homosexuality? Abortion? Name it. Be honest with yourself.

Caring qualifies you as an *instrument of healing.* What makes you cry is a clue to a problem God has anointed you to change, conquer and heal. Look at Nehemiah. His heart was broken about the walls of Jerusalem being broken down. He could not sleep at night. He could not rest. He wept long hours.

He was stirred with everything within him to write letters, connect with officials and even change his personal life to rebuild the walls.

Examine Ezra. His heart was broken over the temple in that city of Jerusalem. He could not rest. He wept and sobbed. He read Scriptures to the people. He knew that the *presence of God was the only remedy for wounded people.* He recognized that places mattered and that God would honor and reward those who sanctified a worship center in the city. *Those feelings were signposts to his Assignment.*

There is an insanity in our society. Observe how the liquor industry has their signs on every billboard of a stadium. Every newspaper is filled with liquor advertisements. Yet alcohol has murdered and destroyed more people on our streets and highways than those killed in the entire Vietnam war.

Someone has said that we have lost more of our children to death by alcoholism than every death combined in all the major wars. Yet, everyone screams about the horrors of war while sipping their alcohol at a cocktail table.

Someday, God is going to raise up another Billy Sunday or someone who is tired of crying over children's brains splattered on a highway. Someone is going to be so grieved over senseless deaths that their Assignment becomes clear. Then, that Assignment *will become an obsession* and that person will rise up to launch a war that will *salvage* the lives of thousands and *heal the broken* in this generation.

Have you wept long hours over financial bankruptcy and debt? Think of the many families in America who lack finances because of a father's drinking habit. Think of the children who cannot be put through school because money is wasted on alcohol. Do you weep when you see the homeless children? *Tears are clues to where God will use you the most.*

Oh, there are many things that should set us on fire. What *grieves* you? What *saddens* you? What moves you to tears? Pay attention to it. *Tears are clues* to the nature of your Assignment.

Where you hurt the most is a clue to what you may heal the best.

"But by the grace of God I am what I am: and His grace which was bestowed upon me was not in vain; but I laboured more abundantly than they all: yet not I, but the grace of God which was with me," (1 Corinthians 15:10).

"For out of much affliction and anguish of heart I wrote unto you with many tears; not that ye should be grieved, but that ye might know the love which I have more abundantly unto you," (2 Corinthians 2:4).

What grieves you is a clue to your Assignment on earth.

❧ Deuteronomy 2:3 ❧

"You have compassed this mountain long enough: turn you northward."

≈ 16 ≈

YOUR ASSIGNMENT IS GEOGRAPHICAL

Places Matter.

God made places before He made people. Therefore, *where* you are is almost as important as what you are.

Some time ago a minister friend shared an interesting story at lunch. "Mike," he said, "when I was 100 miles away from Dallas, I had fair success but nothing extraordinary. The moment I moved to Dallas, our church here absolutely exploded. I knew immediately that I was at the right place at the *right* time."

Where You Are Determines What Grows Within You. Your weaknesses or your strengths require a *climate* to grow.

God spoke to Moses. "You have compassed this mountain long enough: turn you northward," (Deuteronomy 2:3).

Jesus knew that *geography mattered.* "And He must needs go through Samaria," (John 4:4). He could have added, "Because there is a woman there who needs Me, who will reach the entire city!" Read John 4:1-42 carefully. Jesus knew that one person was in need of Him that very day.

Jonah was instructed to go to Nineveh. He rebelled. The whole world has since read his diary of attending

"Whale University!"

Abraham was instructed to *leave* his father's house in Ur of the Chaldees and set out for a *new land*.

Ruth left Moab and followed her mother-in-law Naomi *back to Bethlehem*, where she met her Boaz!

Esther was raised by Mordecai. But when God got ready to bless her, He moved *her into the palace*.

Five hundred were instructed by Jesus to go to the *Upper Room*. Only 120 obeyed. Only 120 got the promised blessing.

You cannot work on the wrong job, for the wrong boss, doing the wrong things for 40 hours a week and wonder why two hours per week in church does not change your life! *Geography plays a major part in every success story.*

God will not bless you just anywhere you go. God will bless you, however, if you are willing to go *anywhere* in order to *obey and please Him!*

Yes it is true: Where You Are Determines What Grows Within You—weeds or flowers, strengths or weaknesses.

Have you noticed that when you are in the presence of certain friends you laugh at different jokes? Have you noticed that the topic of your conversation often changes, *depending on the people* you are around?

2 Keys That Have Unlocked Miracles For My Own Life

▶ *Where You Are Determines Who Sees You.*
▶ *Those Who See You Determine The Favor That Comes Toward You.*
Nobody receives favor unless he is SEEN. Joseph

did not get promoted until Pharaoh *saw* him. Ruth did not get promoted until Boaz *saw* her. The blind man received no instructions for healing until Jesus *saw* him. The daughter of Pharaoh did not show favor to baby Moses in the basket until she *saw* him.

Geography matters. It controls the *flow of favor* in your life. And never forget that *one day of favor is worth a thousand days of labor.*

Go Where You Are Celebrated Instead of Where You Are Tolerated. Seek to be where God wants you, daily, hourly, weekly. Become more conscious of where you *are*, where you *work* and *for whom* you work.

It is so sad that some people simply take a newspaper and start calling places looking for a job instead of sitting in the presence of God and asking Him, *"To whom have I been sent today?"* Somebody is supposed to succeed *because of you.* Who is it? To *whom* have you been *sent?*

You see, *when you are with the right people, the best comes out of you* and the worse part of you will die.

Your success is always linked to a PLACE: the place of your Assignment.

∼ Acts 7:22-23 ∼

"And Moses was learned in all the
Wisdom of the Egyptians, and was mighty
in words and in deeds. And when he was
full forty years old, it came into his heart to
visit his brethren the children of Israel."

❧ 17 ❧

YOUR ASSIGNMENT WILL REQUIRE SEASONS OF PREPARATION

You Are Not Born Qualified, You Must Become Qualified.

Look at the life of Moses. He spent his first 40 years learning the Wisdom of the Egyptians. "And Moses was learned in all the Wisdom of the Egyptians, and was mighty in words and in deeds. And when he was full forty years old, it came into his heart to visit his brethren the children of Israel," (Acts 7:22-23).

He spent another 40 years learning the lessons of leadership and priesthood. "Now Moses kept the flock of Jethro his father in law, the priest of Midian: and he led the flock to the backside of the desert, and came to the mountain of God, even to Horeb," (Exodus 3:1).

"...when forty years were expired, there appeared to him in the wilderness of mount Sina an angel of the Lord in a flame of fire in a bush. When Moses saw it, he wondered at the sight: and as he drew near to behold it, the voice of the Lord came unto him," (Acts 7:30-31).

Moses was a protégé for 80 years. His first 40 years, he was a general in the Egyptian army. His second 40 years, he was a shepherd of hundreds of sheep.

Preparation. *Preparation.* PREPARATION.

Jesus spent 30 years preparing for his ministry. "And Jesus Himself began to be about thirty years of age," (Luke 3:23). These days seem so different for young ministers. The average young minister wants to prepare for 3 and one-half years for 30 years of public ministry. Jesus did the opposite. *He prepared for 30 years for a public ministry of 3 and one-half years.*

The Apostle Paul was a Pharisee and the son of a Pharisee. (Read Acts 23:6.) He had invested years in preparation for the intelligentsia of his generation. "If any other man thinketh that he hath whereof he might trust in the flesh, I more: Circumcised the eighth day, of the stock of Israel, of the tribe of Benjamin, an Hebrew of the Hebrews; as the touching the law, a Pharisee; Concerning zeal, persecuting the church; touching the righteousness which is in the law, blameless," (Philippians 3:4-6).

Yet, that was not enough preparation. "But what things were gain to me, those I counted loss for Christ," (verse 7).

God had another 3 year school for him. "Neither went I up to Jerusalem to them which were apostles before me; but I went into Arabia, and returned again unto Damascus. Then after three years I went up to Jerusalem to see Peter, and abode with him fifteen days," (Galatians 1:17-18).

Paul mentored others concerning various seasons of life in the ministry.

14 Seasons Every Uncommon Minister Will Experience

1. Seasons of Affliction—"...but be thou partaker of the afflictions of the gospel according to the power of God," (2 Timothy 1:8). "It is good for me that I have been afflicted: that I might learn Thy statutes," (Psalm 119:71).

2. Seasons of Solitude—"Greatly desiring to see thee, being mindful of thy tears, that I may be filled with joy," (2 Timothy 1:4).

3. Seasons of Warfare—"Thou therefore endure hardness, as a good soldier of Jesus Christ. No man that warreth entangleth himself with the affairs of this life; that he may please Him who hath chosen him to be a soldier," (2 Timothy 2:3-4).

4. Seasons of Suffering—"If we suffer, we shall also reign with Him: if we deny Him, He will also deny us," (2 Timothy 2:12).

5. Seasons of Ignorance—"Study to shew thyself approved unto God, a workman that needeth not to be ashamed, rightly dividing the word of truth," (2 Timothy 2:15).

6. Seasons of Carnal Desire—"Flee also youthful lusts: but follow righteousness, faith, charity, peace, with them that call on the Lord out of a pure heart," (2 Timothy 2:22).

7. Seasons of Contention—"But foolish and unlearned questions avoid, knowing that they do gender strifes. And the servant of the Lord must not strive; but be gentle unto all men, apt to teach, patient," (2 Timothy 2:23-24).

8. Seasons of Persecution—"Persecutions,

afflictions, which came unto me...what persecutions I
endured: but out of them all the Lord delivered me.
Yea, and all that will live godly in Christ Jesus shall
suffer persecution," (2 Timothy 3:11-12).

9. **Seasons of Proving Yourself**—"But watch
thou in all things, and endure afflictions, do the work of
an evangelist, make full proof of thy ministry,"
(2 Timothy 4:5).

10. **Seasons of Disloyalty**—"For Demas hath
forsaken me, having loved this present world, and is
departed unto Thessalonica," (2 Timothy 4:10).

11. **Seasons of Injustice**—"Alexander the
coppersmith did me much evil: the Lord reward him
according to his works," (2 Timothy 4:14).

12. **Seasons of Isolation**—"At my first answer
no man stood with me, but all men forsook me: I pray
God that it may not be laid to their charge," (2 Timothy
4:16).

13. **Seasons of Supernatural Intervention**—
"Notwithstanding the Lord stood with me, and
strengthened me; that by me the preaching might be
fully known, and that all the Gentiles might hear,"
(2 Timothy 4:17).

14. **Seasons of Deliverance**—"I was delivered
out of the mouth of the lion. And the Lord shall deliver
me from every evil work, and will preserve me until His
Heavenly kingdom: to whom be glory for ever and
ever," (2 Timothy 4:17-18).

In every season, he walked in VICTORY. (See
Romans 8:35-39.)

As I review the more than 60 years of my life, I see
many seasons. In each season, I felt ignorant and
unaware of the *purpose* of that specific season. I would

wonder, "How can God get any glory out of this situation?" Looking back, I see His Divine intervention. He has taught me so much.

Did you ever see the movie, "The Karate Kid?" It contains some powerful lessons. The young boy desperately wanted to learn the art of fighting. His old mentor waited. Instead, he handed him a paint brush and instructed him to paint the fence. The young man was so disheartened. But, he followed the instructions of his mentor.

Discouraged, disillusioned and very disappointed, he could not see any relationship between painting the fence and fighting in the ring. When he finished, he was instructed to polish the car. As he moved his hands in a circular motion over the car, he was very demoralized. His thoughts were, "How will this help me in my future desire to be a great fighter?" But, the old mentor was secretly preparing each motion of his hands to *develop the hands of a fighter.* The young man did not discern it until much later.

Your Heavenly Father knows what He is doing with your life. "But He knoweth the way that I take: when He hath tried me, I shall come forth as gold," (Job 23:10).

Sometimes you will not discern His presence. "Behold, I go forward, but He is not there; and backward, but I cannot perceive Him: On the left hand, where He doth work, but I cannot behold Him: He hideth Himself on the right hand, that I cannot see him," (Job 23:8-9).

Yes, you will even experience seasons of chastening. "For whom the Lord loveth He chasteneth, and scourgeth every son whom He receiveth...Now no chastening for the present seemeth to be joyous, but grievous: nevertheless afterward it yieldeth the peaceable fruit of righteousness unto them which are exercised thereby," (Hebrews 12:6, 11).

Embrace fully and have expectation of the present season God has scheduled in your life. Extract every possible benefit. "Wherefore lift up the hands which hang down, and the feeble knees," (Hebrews 12:12).

You will survive the fires of the furnace. "Though I walk in the midst of trouble, Thou wilt revive me: Thou shalt stretch forth Thine hand against the wrath of mine enemies, and Thy right hand shall save me," (Psalm 138:7).

You are being perfected for your Assignment. "The Lord will perfect that which concerneth me," (Psalm 138:8).

Your success is inevitable.

≈ 18 ≈

YOUR ASSIGNMENT MAY BE MISUNDERSTOOD BY THOSE CLOSEST TO YOU

What Becomes Familiar Often Becomes Hidden.
Let me explain. Suppose you have driven every morning to your job for the last 5 years. You see the *same* buildings, *same* stores and the *same* places of business. Suddenly, you note something. You see a new sign and store.

"When did they build that?" you exclaimed!

"That's always been there," comes the puzzled reply of your friend. It's true. That building and sign had been there for several years. But, *it became so familiar to you that your mind began to ignore it.*

6 Insights To Remember When Your Family Does Not Understand Your Assignment

1. **What Becomes Familiar To The Mind, The Mind Makes A Decision To Ignore.** It wants something new and different. So for whatever reason, something wakes up your interest.

Our families experience this. You have been around your brothers and sisters so long that their outstanding *qualities* have become familiar, and *now hidden* to you. Others respond and compliment them. You do not respond to those qualities any longer *because you have become accustomed to them.*

2. **Intellect, Communication Skills And Integrity Do Not Necessarily Guarantee Your Acceptance.** Demas traveled with Paul. How could the gospel through the greatness and tenacity of Paul become common place? But, it *did.* The newness and magnetism of the gospel became *too familiar,* "For Demas hath forsaken me, having loved this present world, and is departed unto Thessalonica," (2 Timothy 4:10).

3. **Jesus Tasted The Bitterness of Familiarity.** He tasted loneliness and alienation from his own brothers. They became so familiar and accustomed to His presence, it was difficult for them to grasp His *divinity* and *significance.* "For neither did His brethren believe in Him," (John 7:5).

4. **You Must Stay Aware of Your Difference From Others.** Jesus did. "My time is not yet come: but your time is alway ready," (John 7:6).

5. **Others Are Not Feeling Your Pain, Your Difference And Your Alienation.** You may even become the target of scorn and ridicule. Jesus knew they did not feel His pain. "The world cannot hate you; but Me it hateth, because I testify of it, that the works thereof are evil," (John 7:7).

6. **Your Family Is Comfortable With Places You Are Not.** Jesus experienced this, too. His brothers were comfortable in places where He was not. "Go ye up unto this feast: I go not up yet unto this feast; for My time is not yet full come," (John 7:8). *You, too, must*

learn to accept this. Otherwise, you can become bitter, angry and retaliatory *when those closest to you seem disloyal and disinterested.* "A prophet is not without honour, but in his own country, and among his own kin, and in his own house," (Mark 6:4).

I have often wished I could attend the "Joseph Workshop." What were the greatest principles that enabled him to *maintain his focus after his own family despised him?* He told his brothers about his remarkable dream.

His father *rebuked* him.

His brothers *envied* him.

He knew *rejection.* "And he told it to his father, and to his brethren: and his father rebuked him, and said unto him, What is this dream that thou hast dreamed? Shall I and thy mother and thy brethren indeed come to bow down ourselves to thee to the earth? And his brethren envied him; but his father observed the saying," (Genesis 37:10-11).

They hated his very presence. He *wanted* to be around them. He *sought* them out. He wanted *conversation.* But, "...when they saw him afar off, even before he came near unto them, they conspired against him to slay him," (Genesis 37:18).

What made them so angry? He was just their kid brother.

Was it his *appearance?* Was it his *behavior* and conduct? *Of course not.* What was their source of agitation? The answer lies clearly seen in their conversation *about* him. "And they said one to another, Behold, this dreamer cometh," (Genesis 37:19).

He had a dream.

▶ They were intimidated by his *dreams.*

► They were angered by his *future.*
► They were uncomfortable with his *destiny.*
► They were infuriated by his *goals.*
► They misunderstood his *Assignment.*

Their minds were too small for the bigness of His future.

Read their words: "Come now therefore, let us slay him, and cast him into the sandpit, and we will say, Some evil beast hath devoured him," (Genesis 37:20).

They were willing to *scheme.*

They were willing to *lie.*

They were willing to *kill.*

It was his dreams that agitated, infuriated and angered them? Keep reading. "...and we shall see what will become of his dreams," (Genesis 37:20).

Destiny is *invisible.*

Greatness is *invisible.*

Yet, *its presence is so powerful that others cannot reject it.* The greatness and destiny of your dream cannot be refuted, doubted or destroyed by hatred. *Greatness has a presence.* Destiny is a magnet. Greatness intimidates. Destiny intimidates.

Look at David. He had been tending sheep. His father wanted him to bring a lunch to his brothers in battle. Were they happy to see him? Were they thrilled because their young brother came to the war? "And Eliab his eldest brother heard when he spake unto the men; and Eliab's anger was kindled against David, and he said, Why camest thou down hither? and with whom hast thou left those few sheep in the wilderness? I know thy pride and the naughtiness of thine heart; for thou art come down that thou mightest see the battle," (1 Samuel 17:28).

What really angered his brother? "And Eliab his eldest brother heard *when he spake unto the men,*" (1 Samuel 17:28). Whatever David said to the other soldiers birthed a volcano of fury from his oldest brother. David had been asking about the rewards offered to a champion of Israel who would defeat Goliath.

David was discussing the blessings, benefits and incentives for champions. *He wanted something in his future more than they really did.* Destiny is in your difference.

► Destiny is in your real difference from others.
► Your difference often *agitates* others.
► Your difference is in the greatness you want to birth in your *future*.
► That difference makes others uncomfortable, miserable and angry in your presence.

Your family is the testing ground of the dreams and destiny God plants within you. You cannot really run away from your family. *Blood does bond.* God made it so. You may experience anger, disappointment and fury. But, for some unexplainable reason, you always *reach back for those in your household* in times of crisis, loss or tragedy.

Adversity can make you more articulate. You are forced to explain what you *feel*, what you *see* and what you *believe* in the face of those who are unbelieving. You are forced to *keep yourself motivated* in the presence of those uninspired. You are forced to grow Seeds of Faith in a climate of *doubt*.

Those closest to you are simply preparing you to become powerful on the field of battle, in the Arena of your Destiny.

So, sharpen your skills. *Listen* closely to their observations. *Consider* their criticisms. God always uses time to vindicate you. Rest in that.

Sometimes the ones closest to you are the last to grasp what you are really about.

Your family is your first classroom in the pursuit of greatness.

≈ **19** ≈

YOUR ASSIGNMENT WILL ALWAYS HAVE AN ENEMY

Someone Will Hate You.
Get used to it.
Your Assignment is to build something that is good and tear down something bad. Listen to the instructions of God to Jeremiah. "See, I have this day set thee over the nations and over the kingdoms, to root out, and to pull down, and to destroy, and to throw down, to build, and to plant," (Jeremiah 1:10).

It is only natural for you to have an enemy. "If the world hate you, ye know that it hated Me before it hated you. If ye were of the world, the world would love his own: but because ye are not of the world, but I have chosen you out of the world, therefore the world hateth you. Remember the word that I said unto you, The servant is not greater than his lord. If they have persecuted Me, they will also persecute you; if they have kept My saying, they will keep yours also. But all these things will they do unto you for My name's sake," (John 15:18-21).

It is an agonizing and heartrending picture, but it happened. After 33 and a-half years on earth, the last moments of Jesus were still *like a magnet to His enemies.* That is why He prayed, "Father, forgive them; for they know not what they do."

Listen to what they were doing around Him: "And the people stood beholding. And the rulers also with them derided Him, saying, He saved others; let Him save himself, if He be Christ, the chosen of God. And the soldiers also mocked Him, coming to Him, and offering Him vinegar, And saying, If thou be the king of the Jews, save thyself...And one of the malefactors which were hanged railed on him, saying, If thou be Christ, save thyself and us," (Luke 23:35-37, 39).

5 Reasons Your Assignment Will Always Have An Enemy

1. Your Assignment Will Stop Something Wrong From Growing Bigger. Esther knew this. (Read Esther 4:13-17.)

2. Your Assignment Will Paralyze The Influence of The Ungodly. Jonah finally embraced this command. "So Jonah arose, and went unto Nineveh, according to the word of the Lord. Now Nineveh was an exceeding great city of three days' journey. And Jonah began to enter into the city a day's journey, and he cried, and said, Yet forty days, and Nineveh shall be overthrown. So the people of Nineveh believed God, and proclaimed a fast, and put on sackcloth, from the greatest of them even to the least of them," (Jonah 3:3-5).

3. Your Assignment Ultimately Will Destroy Something God Hates Very Much. David knew this. (Read 1 Samuel 17:45-53.)

4. Your Assignment Will Grow Something Significant In Another. David knew this. (Read 1 Samuel 17:52.)

5. Your Assignment Will Strengthen Something Satan Wants To Keep Weakened. Aaron and Hur experienced this. (Read Exodus 17:12.)

3 Mistakes Your Enemy Will Always Make

1. Your Enemy Will Always Misinterpret The Events Around You. (Read Matthew 27:40-44.)

2. What They Assume Is Your End Will Always Be Your Birthing And Beginning. (Read Job 2:3-7; 42:10, 12, 17.)

3. What Your Enemy Assumes Is Your Exit From Their Presence Is Actually Your Entry Into Your Next Season of Promotion. (Read Acts 7:54-59.)

7 Secrets Every Survivor Must Know

1. As Long As You Live, There Will Be An Adversary To Oppose You At Every Turn. So, learning spiritual warfare against satanic forces is important—it is absolutely necessary.

2. You Must Learn That Satan Is Your Only True Enemy. "For we wrestle not against flesh and blood, but against principalities, against powers, against the rulers of the darkness of this world, against spiritual wickedness in high places," (Ephesians 6:12).

3. Your Sufficiency Is Not In Yourself. "Not that we are sufficient of ourselves to think anything as of ourselves; but our sufficiency is of God; Who also hath made us able ministers of the new testament," (2 Corinthians 3:5-6).

4. You Must Decide To Fight Back. "Finally,

my brethren, be strong in the Lord, and in the power of His might," (Ephesians 6:10). It is your personal responsibility to stand against the methods of satan against you. "Put on the whole armour of God, that ye may be able to stand against the wiles of the devil," (Ephesians 6:11).

5. You Must Decide To Put On The Spiritual Armor That Protects And Defends You. "Wherefore take unto you the whole armour of God, that ye may be able to withstand in the evil day, and having done all, to stand. Stand therefore, having your loins girt about with truth, and having on the breastplate of righteousness; And your feet shod with the preparation of the gospel of peace; Above all, taking the shield of faith, wherewith ye shall be able to quench all the fiery darts of the wicked. And take the helmet of salvation, and the sword of the Spirit, which is the word of God: Praying always with all prayer and supplication in the Spirit, and watching thereunto with all perseverance and supplication for all saints," (Ephesians 6:13-18).

6. You Must Be Teachable And Capable of Being Mentored Daily By The Holy Spirit To The Techniques of Warfare. "Blessed be the Lord my strength, which teacheth my hands to war, and my fingers to fight," (Psalm 144:1).

7. Remind Yourself About The Rewards of Overcoming. "He that overcometh, the same shall be clothed in white raiment; and I will not blot out his name out of the book of life, but I will confess his name before My Father, and before His angels," (Revelation 3:5). "Him that overcometh will I make a pillar in the temple of My God, and he shall go no more out: and I will write upon him the name of My God, and the name of the city of My God, which is new Jerusalem, which cometh down out of Heaven from My God: and I will write upon him My new name," (Revelation 3:12).

"To him that overcometh will I grant to sit with Me in My throne, even as I also overcame, and am sat down with My Father in His throne," (Revelation 3:21).

▶ Satan wants your focus to be on the Battle.

▶ God wants your focus to be on the *Spoils* of Battle.

Remember That Battle Is When Two Forces Want The Same Possession. So, your purpose in your Assignment is not merely survival in the heat of battle. Your battle is to win you possession of something you desperately desire, need and deserve.

The persistent win. Always.

Your Assignment will attract criticism and your anointing will attract attack.

Somebody will not like what you are doing. Ever.

22 Defense Techniques To Remember During Seasons of Personal Attack

1. Expect Someone To Be Unhappy Over Your Progress. They always are. They "hired counsellors against them, to frustrate their purpose," (Ezra 4:5). Letters were written. Accusations were believed.

Read it for yourself. "Now when the copy of king Artaxerxes' letter was read before Rehum, and Shimshai the scribe, and their companions, they went up in haste to Jerusalem unto the Jews, and made them to cease by force and power. Then ceased the work of the house of God which is at Jerusalem," (Ezra 4:23-24).

2. Remember That You Are A Champion, Not A Loser.

▶ Champions spend their time building their dream.

▶ Losers spend their life criticizing it.

3. Invest Your Words And Energy In Creating New Goals And Dreams. Losers invest their words and labor trying to destroy the goals of others. "Let no corrupt communication proceed out of your mouth, but that which is good to the use of edifying, that it may minister grace unto the hearers. And grieve not the Holy Spirit of God, whereby ye are sealed unto the day of redemption. Let all bitterness, and wrath, and anger, and clamour, and evil speaking, be put away from you, with all malice," (Ephesians 4:29-31).

4. Recognize That What Makes You Weep Will Cause Others To Become Angry. Nehemiah wept over the condition of Jerusalem. "...the wall of Jerusalem also is broken down, and the gates thereof are burned with fire. And it came to pass, when I heard these words, that I sat down and wept, and mourned certain days, and fasted, and prayed before the God of Heaven," (Nehemiah 1:3-4).

5. Remember That When Your Assignment Is Awakened Within You, Your Adversary Is Awakened Against You. It happened to Nehemiah. "When Sanballat the Horonite, and Tobiah the servant, the Ammonite, heard of it, it grieved them exceedingly that there was come a man to seek the welfare of the children of Israel...they laughed us to scorn, and despised us...they were very wroth, And conspired all of them together to come and to fight against Jerusalem, and to hinder it," (Nehemiah 2:10, 19; 4:7-8).

6. Pray, Confess, Weep And Cast Yourself Down Before God. "Now when Ezra had prayed, and when he had confessed, weeping and casting himself down before the house of God, there assembled unto him out of Israel a very great congregation of men and women and children: for the people wept very sore," (Ezra 10:1).

7. Fast. Ezra did. "Then Ezra rose up from before the house of God...and when he came thither, he did eat no bread, nor drink water," (Ezra 10:6).

8. Exhort Those Working Around You To Be Strong And Unafraid And To Be Willing To Fight For Their Families. Ezra did. "And I looked, and rose up, and said unto the nobles, and to the rulers, and to the rest of the people, Be not ye afraid of them: remember the Lord, which is great and terrible, and fight for your brethren, your sons, and your daughters, your wives, and your houses," (Nehemiah 4:14).

9. Stay Awake, Alert And Aware. Nehemiah did. "Nevertheless we made our prayer unto our God, and set a watch against them day and night, because of them," (Nehemiah 4:9).

10. Stay Productive And Focused. Nehemiah did. "...we returned all of us to the wall, every one unto his work," (Nehemiah 4:15).

11. Rearrange Your Daily Routine In Order To Keep Cautious, Guarded And Protected From Your Enemies. "So neither I, nor my brethren, nor my servants, nor the men of the guard which followed me, none of us put off our clothes, saving that every one put them off for washing," (Nehemiah 4:23).

12. Encourage Singers And Spiritual Leaders To Be At Their Place of Assignment. Nehemiah did. "Now it came to pass, when the wall was built, and I had set up the doors, and the porters and the singers and the Levites were appointed," (Nehemiah 7:1).

13. Secure The Leadership And Management Skills of Faithful, Godly Men. "That I gave my brother Hanani, and Hananiah the ruler of the palace, charge over Jerusalem: for he was a faithful man, and feared God above many," (Nehemiah 7:2).

14. Study The Biographies of Those Who Have Endured. Paul experienced much attack and criticism. "Alexander the coppersmith did me much evil: the Lord reward him according to his works: Of whom be thou ware also," (2 Timothy 4:14-15).

15. Forgive Those Who Attack You, Knowing That God Will Stand With You. "At my first answer no man stood with me, but all men forsook me: I pray God that it may not be laid to their charge. Notwithstanding the Lord stood with me, and strengthened me; that by me the preaching might be fully known, and that all the Gentiles might hear: and I was delivered out of the mouth of the lion," (2 Timothy 4:16-17).

16. Stay Focused On Your Assignment. Paul stayed focused on the results of his ministry and kept his expectation up and God as his deliverer. "And the Lord shall deliver me from every evil work, and will preserve me unto His Heavenly kingdom," (2 Timothy 4:18).

17. Pursue The Presence of God And His Word. David did. When David was attacked and criticized, he pursued the presence of God and absorbed the words of the covenant. "Unless thy law had been my delights, I should then have perished in mine affliction," (Psalm 119:92).

18. Develop More Wisdom Regarding The Purpose of Attack.

▶ Criticism is an attack designed to *distract* you.

▶ Attack is opposition designed to *destroy* you.

▶ Criticism is intended to *demoralize* you.

▶ Attack is intended to demoralize *those around you,* anyone desiring to help you.

▶ Criticism is meant to make your future *undesirable.*

▶ Attack is to make your future *unreachable.*

▶ Critics will oppose your *methods.*

▶ Adversaries fear your *motives.*

19. Remember That Your Attitude Is More Important Than The Attack Against You. Attacks pass. Your attitude, if bitter or demoralized, *can grow a root of bitterness within you* that will poison every day of your *future.* "Looking diligently lest any man fail of the grace of God; lest any root of bitterness springing up trouble you, and thereby many be defiled," (Hebrews 12:15).

20. Secure The Ministry of An Intercessor. "That if two of you shall agree on earth as touching any thing that they shall ask, it shall be done for them of My Father which is in Heaven," (Matthew 18:19).

21. Expect Your Faith To Be Honored Supernaturally By The God That Intervenes, Just When You Need It The Most. "And Jesus answering saith unto them, Have faith in God. For verily I say unto to you, That whosoever shall say unto this mountain, Be thou removed, and be thou cast into the sea; and shall not doubt in his heart, but shall believe that those things which he saith shall come to pass; he shall have whatsoever he saith. Therefore I say unto you, What things soever ye desire, when ye pray, believe that ye receive them, and ye shall have them," (Mark 11:22-24).

22. Expect God To Bring The Counsel of Your Enemies To Nought. "And it came to pass, when our enemies heard that it was known unto us, and God had brought their counsel to nought, that we returned all of us to the wall, every one unto his work," (Nehemiah 4:15).

8 Keys That Unlock Victory In Every Attack

1. Attack Reveals That Your Enemy Fully Believes You Are Capable of Obtaining Your Goal. They would not waste their ammunition, time, finances and effort if they thought your dreams or goals were impossible. "I can do all things through Christ which strengtheneth me," (Philippians 4:13). If your *enemy* believes in your *future*, so should *you*.

2. Satan Only Attacks At The Birth of Something Significant In Your Life. It may be your ministry, like Jesus in Matthew 4; it may be the birth of a champion in your household, like the birth of Moses that activated the killing of all the new born children in Egypt; it may be the birth of a miracle about to occur in your personal life. (See Daniel 9.)

3. Satan Uses Those Closest To You As Gates Into Your Heart. Your intercession is often the *only covering* they have so pray daily for the grace and mercies of God to be shown toward *those you love.* "And a man's foes shall be they of his own household," (Matthew 10:36).

4.   The Word of God Is The Best Defense You Possess. Jesus used it in Matthew 4 during His temptation season.   It will work every time to demoralize the tirade of words satan uses relentlessly against your mind. "Unless Thy law had been my delights, I should then have perished in mine affliction," (Psalm 119:92).

5.   Angels Are Continuously Ready To Minister To You At The Conclusion of A Crisis. "Then the devil leaveth Him, and, behold, angels came and ministered unto Him," (Matthew 4:11).

6.   Continuous Praise And Worship Leaving Your Lips Demoralizes Satan And Attracts The Presence of God. "I will bless the Lord at all times: His praise shall continually be in my mouth," (Psalm 34:1).

7.   Your Faith Is Working For You Every Moment of Your Life.   "But without faith it is impossible to please Him: for he that cometh to God must believe that He is, and that He is a rewarder of them that diligently seek Him," (Hebrews 11:6).

8.   The Weapon of Wisdom Assures Your Promotion Will Follow Every Crisis. "If we suffer, we shall also reign with Him: if we deny Him, He also will deny us," (2 Timothy 2:12). "For Wisdom is a defence, and money is a defence: but the excellency of knowledge is, that Wisdom giveth life to them that have it," (Ecclesiastes 7:12).

Attack is merely proof that your enemy considers your Assignment achievable.

≈ 2 Timothy 2:15 ≈

"Study to shew thyself approved unto God, a
workman that needeth not to be ashamed,
rightly dividing the word of truth."

∾ 20 ∾

YOU WILL ONLY SUCCEED WHEN YOUR ASSIGNMENT BECOMES AN OBSESSION

Focus Is Magnetic.

When you give your attention, time and total effort to achieving your Assignment, you will experience extraordinary currents of favor and miracles. *Whatever has the ability to keep your attention has mastered you.*

Jesus Himself rebuked those who attempted to break His focus and obsession for completing the will of the Father. "But when He had turned about and looked on His disciples, He rebuked Peter, saying, Get thee behind me, satan: for thou savourest not the things that be of God, but the things that be of men," (Mark 8:33).

The Apostle Paul was obsessed with his Assignment. It explains his remarkable success in the face of enemies, adversaries and even friends who misunderstood him. It explains his letter to the Philippians, "...this one thing I do, forgetting those things which are behind, and reaching forth unto those things which are before, I press toward the mark for the prize of the high calling of God in Christ Jesus," (Philippians 3:13-14).

He moved *away* from past hurts, failures and

memories. Obviously, he had a *photograph* of those things before him.

8 Keys To Developing An Obsession For Your Assignment

1. Refuse Any Weight or Distraction To Your Assignment. "...let us lay aside every weight, and the sin which doth so easily beset us, and let us run with patience the race that is set before us," (Hebrews 12:1).

2. Be Ruthless In Severing Any Ties To A Project or Person Not Connected To God's Assignment. He instructed Timothy, "No man that warreth entangleth himself with the affairs of this life; that he may please Him who hath chosen him to be a soldier," (2 Timothy 2:4).

3. Constantly Study Your Assignment. He urged Timothy, "Study to shew thyself approved unto God, a workman that needeth not to be ashamed, rightly dividing the word of truth," (2 Timothy 2:15).

4. Shun Conversations That Are Unrelated To Your Assignment. "But shun profane and vain babblings: for they will increase unto more ungodliness...But foolish and unlearned questions avoid, knowing that they do gender strifes," (2 Timothy 2:16, 23).

5. Learn To Disconnect From Any Relationship That Does Not Feed Your Addiction To His Presence And Obsession To Complete God's Assignment In Your Life. "And if any man obey not our word by this epistle, note that man, and have no company with him, that he may be ashamed," (2 Thessalonians 3:14).

Satan *dreads* the *completion* of your Assignment. Each act of obedience can destroy a thousand satanic plans and desires.

6. **When You Insist On Building Your Life Around Your Assignment, Wrong Relationships Die.** Right relationships thrive. I have said it a thousand times that the best way to disconnect from wrong people is to become obsessed with doing the right thing.

7. **When Your Obsession Is Doing The Right Thing, Wrong People Find You Unbearable.** It is permissible for others to share their dreams with me. It is disappointing to discover that they want nothing to do with you nor your Assignment. It is rewarding to know that the Father will reward you a hundredfold for *your obsession* to do what His plan is for your life. (Read Mark 10:28-30.)

8. **Fight For Your Focus.** Battle hard. Build walls that strengthen your concentration. Ignore the jeers, laughter and criticism that you are "obsessed."

You Will Only Succeed When Your Assignment Becomes An Obsession.

≈ Proverbs 18:16 ≈

"A man's gift maketh room for him, and
bringeth him before great men."

Section 3

THE SEED

❧ 1 Kings 17:14-15 ❧

"For thus saith the Lord God of Israel, The barrel of meal shall not waste, neither shall the cruse of oil fail, until the day that the Lord sendeth rain upon the earth. And she went and did according to the saying of Elijah: and she, and he, and her house, did eat many days."

≈ 21 ≈

INVENTORY THE SEEDS YOU ALREADY POSSESS

A Seed Is A Tiny Beginning With A Huge Future.
It is anything that can become more. It is the *Beginning*. It is anything you can *do, know or possess* that could bless somebody else.

Your *Thoughts* are Seeds for desired behavior, conduct and creativity.

Your *Love* is a Seed.

Your *Time* is a Seed.

Your *Patience* is a Seed.

Your *Money* is a Seed.

Your *Kindness* is a Seed.

Your *Prayers* are Seeds.

Stopping slander is a Seed.

Forgiveness is a Seed.

Thankfulness is a Seed.

Your Seed is anything you have received from God that can be traded for something else.

You are a walking *warehouse of Seeds*. Most people do not even know this. They have no idea how many Seeds they contain that can be planted into the lives of others.

▶ Anything that *improves* another is a Seed.

▶ Anything that makes another *smile* is a Seed.

▶ Anything that makes someone's *life easier* is a Seed.

Millions are so busy studying what they do not have that they overlook something they have already received.

Certainly you must inventory your needs. But it is more important to inventory your Seeds. Stop focusing on what you *do not* have, and look closer at something you *already have been given.*

Moses did. He complained that he could not talk. God instructed him to shut up and lift up the rod in his hand. That was his Seed. His tool to create his future.

David complained that he could not use the armor of Saul. God instructed him to look back at the slingshot he possessed. God always gives you something that can *begin* your future.

Something you have been given will create anything else you have been promised.

Little things birth big things. Acorns become oak trees.

One of my associate evangelists has some remarkable qualities that will make him succeed with his life. He is willing to be corrected. He never pouts, never sulks, never withdraws. When he makes a mistake, he is swift to admit it. He does not have a lazy bone in him.

His *golden attitude* is a *golden* Seed.

So, when God provided some extra finances for my ministry, the first thing I wanted to do was to purchase him a suit. Why? His Seeds of kindness, faithfulness and love were working. His Harvest was inevitable.

Most people have no idea about what a Seed really is. Showing up at work on time...is a Seed. Showing up *ahead of time* is another Seed. You see, anything that you can do to make life easier for your boss or anyone else...is a Seed.

Millions have never used 10 percent of the Seed

stored within them. You see, mowing the grass for your church is a Seed. Babysitting for a struggling single parent is a Seed.

You are a living collection of Seeds, a museum of powerful, tiny golden passionate beginnings.

You must recognize your Seed God has stored within you. Your Seed is any gift, skill or talent that God has provided for you to sow into the lives of others around you. Don't hide it. Use your Seed. Celebrate the existence of Seeds in your life...that are carving the road to your future. Even Joseph recognized his ability to interpret dreams. He wanted to help others. When Pharaoh became troubled, Joseph had a Seed to sow toward his life. "A man's gift maketh room for him, and bringeth him before great men," (Proverbs 18:16).

One of the greatest stories in ancient writings is in 1 Kings 17. Elijah was being fed by ravens at the brook, Cherith. When the brook dried up and the raven failed to show, God gave him a new instruction to go to Zarephath, a small village in Zidon. There, a widow would receive an instruction to provide food for them. When he arrived at the widow's, the scene was dismal and tragic. She was out gathering two sticks. (I'll call them two pancakes.) Her son lay emaciated on his deathbed in her little house.

Yet, the man of God spoke boldly to her to plant a Seed and give him some of her food.

Her supply had run out. She had no faith for survival. She had no faith for provision. She is looking at her last meal on earth for her and her son.

Now imagine the instructions from the man of God, "Take one of those pancakes and give it to me." She could have easily said, "Every one of you preachers have been trying to get my pancakes. I got 10 letters this week from television preachers wanting to share this pancake."

But, Elijah starts giving instructions that are Scriptural. His *instructions* are Seeds. He was sowing them toward the widow. "Would you go get some water for me? While you're at it, would you bring me a little meal?"

"I can't do that. I don't have enough for all of us. Just enough for me and my son."

Elijah explained patiently, "I understand that. You're wise to take care of your son. I want you to do that. But, *first* bring something to me as a man of God. Sow it as a beginning, a Seed."

Then, he suddenly gives her a miracle reason *for sowing*. No, he does not pull out his newsletter and show her a photograph of a dead bird who never showed back up to feed him. He made no reference to the brook drying up. He never told her that his ministry was over and he would starve if she did not cook him a meal.

Rather he showed her a picture of a future. Something that she had not noticed. He revealed to her that something she already had in her possession *was the golden key to getting into her future*. He gave her a picture of the potential supply, the Harvest. (Read 1 Kings 17:14.)

You need somebody to help you sow the Seed you possess. You need someone to show you a picture of the future within it.

Develop an appreciation for the man of God who helps you discover your Seed, and provides a photograph of the Harvest you can expect.

Elijah did it. It turned a poor woman into a miracle woman. From poverty to plenty. From famine to supply.

You see, most people have not even noticed something *they already* have that can create their future.

Your *Time* is a Seed. It will produce what money cannot. A friend of mine was brokenhearted. His teenage son had received a car, world travel tickets and still hated his father.

"Change the Seed if you do not like the Harvest you are producing," I said. "Stop the money flow. Provide him two hours a day for 14 days of nonjudgmental time. *Give him what he cannot find anywhere else and he will return to you.* Create a non-critical climate. Permit him to talk and discuss anything with you for two hours a day. Document what occurs." Two weeks later they became best buddies, going fishing in the morning. The crisis was over. *He found a Seed that would produce the desired result.*

Time is a precious thing. *Wherever* you sow it, something incredible will *grow.*

Think of the huge space called eternity. God reached into it and took a chunk of it and placed it on earth, calling it Time. Imagine Him saying, "Here is Time. You can trade it for anything else you want on earth." In a sense, He did not give you friends—He gave you Time. You sowed Time and created strong friendships. God has never "handed" you any money. He gave you Time. You went to someone with money and exchanged your Time for their money. Your boss has money, and you have "Time" in the way of work to trade with.

Time is the currency on earth.

France has the franc. Germany has the marc. Japan has the yen. England has the pound. Mexico has the peso. America has the dollar.

Your currency on earth is Time. God gave you Time to exchange for anything else that was important to you.

I have never met a poor person who was aware of the importance of Time. I have never met a wealthy person who was *not* aware of the importance of Time.

You see, your Time is a precious gift from God.

Your Time is a Seed that can produce what money cannot buy.

Imagine this scenario with me for a moment. You happen to be in the office when your boss leans back in his chair and sighs, "I sure wish I had a good glass of carrot juice." Let me show you a few responses that usually occur:

1. $5.00 an hour employee: "I'd like to have a glass of carrot juice too!"

2. $6.00 an hour employee: "You like carrot juice! I like cokes myself."

3. $7.00 an hour employee: "If I had some carrots, I'd make you some."

4. $8.00 an hour employee: "Would you like for me to find someone to make you some?"

5.   Employee who can eventually decide his own salary: "I will be right back, sir, within 20 minutes." He returns with a glass of carrot juice requesting information. "Would you like this daily at a specific time? It can happen, sir."

That's Seed-*sowing*.

Every time your boss is disappointed, you have a chance to prove your uniqueness and significance. Every time you see him unhappy, it is a door to a promotion. Look, look and *look again* for opportunities to plant a Seed. They are all around you every day. Hundreds of them.

Every Seed is a Golden Door from your present into your future. If you do not recognize a Seed, how could you ever recognize the Harvest from it?

If a farmer has never seen what a kernel of corn

looks like, do you think he would recognize a field of stalks of corn on the side of the road? Of course not. *You cannot begin to recognize a Harvest until you recognize a Seed—something* precious within you God has enabled you to know, do or possess and sow.

You are a Walking Warehouse of Seeds.

Invest Time in The Secret Place, your personal place of prayer. Ask The Holy Spirit to show you what you have been given, supernaturally and naturally to plant into the lives of others. Your future begins in your own hands.

► You can *see* something nobody else can see.

► You *know* something others do not know.

► You see *problems* that others do not see.

Solving them is your Seed that brings any kind of Harvest that you desire.

Millions have no idea what a Seed really is, so they never receive the Harvest from it because it goes unplanted and unsown.

Discover the Seeds you have already received from God and your future can be anything you desire.

RECOMMENDED INVESTMENTS:
Creating Tomorrow Through Seed-Faith (Book/B-06/32 pgs)
The Secret of The Seed (Book/B-129/128 pgs)
My Seed Testimony (Book/B-242/32 pgs)

≈ James 4:2 ≈

"...ye have not, because ye ask not."

✎ **22** ✎

LEARN THE SECRET OF GIVING YOUR SEED A SPECIFIC ASSIGNMENT

━━━━━━━⟫•O•⟪━━━━━━━

Every Seed Contains An Invisible Instruction.
Let me explain. You cannot see it. It is too small and invisible to the natural eye. But, it is obviously there. If you could look deep into the watermelon seed, you would see an invisible instruction that it contains, "produce a watermelon." Tomato seeds contain invisible instruction "produce tomatoes."

There is no wavering or uncertainty. The Seed contains an incredible Assignment. It is precise, exact and specific. The Creator had decided the Harvest when He created the Seed.

When God wanted a family, He sowed His Son. He gave His Son an Assignment to "seek and save that which was lost." Jesus was the best Seed God ever planted on earth. But, He contained an Assignment, an instruction, a purpose. Everything He did was connected to that Assignment.

David must have learned this incredible secret of giving his Seed a specific Assignment. When thousands lay dead across the city, he cried out to God and brought him a *specific offering* for a *specific purpose*. "And David built there an altar unto the Lord, and offered burnt offerings and peace offerings. So the Lord was intreated for the land, and the plague was stayed from Israel," (2 Samuel 24:25).

Elijah taught this incredible Principle of Assignment to the widow of Zarephath. As she was going to bring water, he gave her a specific instruction..."Bring me, I pray thee, a morsel of bread in thine hand."

Then, Elijah did something few ministers ever do. *He gave her a photograph of what that Seed was supposed to produce.* "For thus saith the Lord God of Israel, The barrel of meal shall not waste, neither shall the cruse of oil fail, until the day that the Lord sendeth rain upon the earth," (1 Kings 17:14).

When you give your Seed an Assignment, energy and faith pours into you. You can see beyond the sacrifice of the moment. The widow did. "And she went and did according to the saying of Elijah: and she, and he, and her house, did eat many days," (1 Kings 17:15).

Does it really work? If you sow for a specific reason, toward a Harvest, does it work? It works *if you are doing it in total obedience to the instructions of God.* "And the barrel of meal wasted not, neither did the cruse of oil fail, according to the word of the Lord, which he spake by Elijah," (1 Kings 17:16). Those instructions may be through a servant of God, The Word of God or through the inner voice of The Holy Spirit.

Your Prayers are Seeds, too.

Job *sowed a Prayer of Deliverance* for his 3 friends. What happened? God turned Job's captivity around. Just like David had stopped a tragedy by offering a special offering to the Lord.

Many years ago, I experienced a personal attack.

It was devastating to me emotionally. My mind was fragmented. Inside, my heart was broken and I wanted to die. It was a situation that could have been complicated by any retaliation or attempts of explanation. I flew down to Los Angeles for another crusade on the same day. The next morning, a Sunday, The Holy Spirit gave me a strange instruction. "Plant a *battle* Seed."

I had never heard of such a thing.

Then, I remembered when David had *aimed his Seed like an arrow.* He gave it an Assignment. He focused it for a desired result. And the plague was stayed. (See 2 Samuel 24:25.)

I planted everything I had that day—$3,000. Supernaturally the attack ended as suddenly as it had began. Isn't that wonderful? You always have a Seed that becomes an exit from your present circumstances.

Your Seed is always the door out of trouble. It is anything you do that *helps* another person. Your Seed is anything that *improves the life of someone near you.* It may be the Seed of information, Seed of encouragement or even the Seed of finances. Whatever you plant, you must remember to give your Seed a specific Assignment so that your faith will not waver. "But let him ask in faith, nothing wavering. For he that wavereth is like a wave of the sea driven with the wind and tossed. For let not that man think that he shall receive any thing of the Lord. A double minded man is unstable in all his ways," (James 1:6-8).

Your faith must have a specific instruction. Not two. Not 3. *One.* "This one thing I do," were the words of the great man of God. David cried out, "My heart is fixed," (Psalm 57:7).

Do not waver. Aim your Seed. "...turn not from it to the right hand or to the left, that thou mayest prosper whithersoever thou goest," (Joshua 1:7).

Giving your Seed a specific Assignment strongly impacts your focus. And focus matters. The secret of success is concentration. *The Only Reason Men Fail Is Broken Focus.*

It is a tragic situation that I have observed on many Sunday mornings in churches. The offering is being received. The pastor explains how the offering will be spent, "We really need a roof. The present roof is in need of repair. Will you help us today?"

The people respond. But their Seed has not really received an instruction. It pays the bills, but it does not multiply back in their lives. Why? It has not been *aimed* to create a *specific* Harvest. If the only desired result involved is to pay for the roof, that is accomplished easily, but the Seed-sowers never receive their personal Harvest in return. Sow your Seed *consistently, generously* and always in obedience to the voice of God. Then, wrap your faith around your Seed and point it like an arrow. Enter into a covenant for a specific and desired result in your life.

Thousands fail to do this and never receive the financial Harvest God promised. "...ye have not, because ye ask not," (James 4:2).

Our Prayer Together...

"Father, You gave Jesus, Your best Seed, an Assignment. Now, millions are born again— changed forever—and You are producing the Harvest You desired, a family. Teach us the Principle of Assignment—giving every Seed we sow a specific Assignment. In Jesus' name. Amen."

～ 23 ～

WAIT LONG ENOUGH FOR YOUR SEED TO PRODUCE YOUR DESIRED HARVEST

Time Is The Hidden And Mysterious Ingredient In An Uncommon Harvest.

You see, patience is a Seed, too. "The Lord is good unto them that wait for Him, to the soul that seeketh Him," (Lamentations 3:25).

Your waiting reveals trust. "It is good that a man should both hope and quietly wait for the salvation of the Lord," (Lamentations 3:26).

Your waiting may be painful. But, it is the season between sowing and reaping. That is why the Bible calls it—Seedtime and Harvest. *Time is the season between the Seed and the Harvest.*

"...weeping may endure for a night, but joy cometh in the morning," (Psalm 30:5).

Some of us have lost the Harvest because of the pain of waiting. Waiting is burdensome. It breeds agitation, a critical spirit and leaves you frustrated.

While waiting, words of doubt and unbelief are spoken. This often aborts the *cycle of blessing.* Unthankfulness brings a curse, not a reward. Ingratitude does not inspire God to hasten the Harvest.

It stops the Harvest.

You must be willing to trust God through the seasons of waiting. He has promised a change.

Your *anger* does not intimidate God.

Your *schedule* does not obligate God.

He is God. He will decide when you deserve and qualify for the Harvest. "For My thoughts are not your thoughts, neither are your ways My ways, saith the Lord. For as the Heavens are higher than the earth, so are My ways higher than your ways, and My thoughts than your thoughts," (Isaiah 55:8-9).

He has already promised you Harvest in due season. "For as the rain cometh down, and the snow from Heaven, and returneth not thither, but watereth the earth, and maketh it bring forth and bud, that it may give Seed to the sower, and bread to the eater: So shall My word be that goeth forth out of My mouth: it shall not return unto Me void, but it shall accomplish that which I please, and it shall prosper in the thing whereto I sent it," (Isaiah 55:10-11).

Get excited about your Harvest. "For ye shall go out with joy, and be led forth with peace: the mountains and the hills shall break forth before you into singing, and all the trees of the field shall clap their hands," (Isaiah 55:12).

God will replace every financial disaster with a financial miracle. "Instead of the thorn shall come up the fir tree, and instead of the brier shall come up the myrtle tree: and it shall be to the Lord for a name, for an everlasting sign that shall not be cut off," (Isaiah 55:13).

You must refuse to permit words of discouragement in your mouth. "Fear thou not; for I am with thee: be not dismayed; for I am thy God: I will strengthen thee;

yea, I will help thee; yea, I will uphold thee with the right hand of My righteousness," (Isaiah 41:10).

Those who oppose and battle against your progress, will be confronted by God Himself. "Behold, all they that were incensed against thee shall be ashamed and confounded: they shall be as nothing; and they that strive with thee shall perish," (Isaiah 41:11).

Your enemies shall not succeed against you. "Thou shalt seek them, and shalt not find them, even them that contended with thee: they that war against thee shall be as nothing, and as a thing of nought. For I the Lord thy God will hold thy right hand, saying unto thee, Fear not; I will help thee," (Isaiah 41:12-13).

The Holy Spirit is involved against your enemy. "When the enemy shall come in like a flood, the Spirit of the Lord shall lift up a standard against him," (Isaiah 59:19).

Every scheme, strategy and trap against you shall ultimately fail if you will be patient in waiting. "No weapon that is formed against thee shall prosper; and every tongue that shall rise against thee in judgment thou shalt condemn. This is the heritage of the servants of the Lord, and their righteousness is of Me, saith the Lord," (Isaiah 54:17).

Keep your eyes upon the rewards for waiting. Men fight for a reason—to gain something they want. When David faced Goliath, he was fully aware of the fantastic *benefits* offered to the person who could defeat Goliath. He would have the hand of the king's daughter. He would not have to pay any taxes. So, armed with the inner picture of his success and its rewards, he ran to Goliath to conquer him.

Jesus went to Calvary, fully aware of the resurrection—"for the joy that was set before Him."

Keep focused. The spoils of war are worth the battle and the tormenting season called waiting.

Refuse to sin with your mouth. Your enemy reacts to your words. If you feed him doubt and unbelief, it will energize and motivate him to rise up against you.

Never speak words that encourage your enemy. Your enemy will believe anything you are telling him. If you feed faith words into his ear, he will be demoralized, disappointed and discouraged. If you talk like a victim, he will be encouraged to attack you again and again and again. "Death and life are in the power of the tongue: and they that love it shall eat the fruit thereof," (Proverbs 18:21).

Your words of faith will influence the heart of God. "For by thy words thou shalt be justified, and by thy words thou shalt be condemned," (Matthew 12:37).

While you are waiting, create a climate of gratitude and thanksgiving. "In every thing give thanks: for this is the will of God in Christ Jesus concerning you," (1 Thessalonians 5:18).

Continuously pray in the Spirit throughout the day. "Pray without ceasing," (1 Thessalonians 5:17).

Avoid the temptation to create a backup plan. "Neither give place to the devil," (Ephesians 4:27).

When one of the great explorers came to America, he burned the ships behind him and the soldiers. It made escape impossible. It made exploration a necessity and requirement. His men could not go back. *You cannot plan your success and failure at the same time.* Your success will require your total focus and attention.

Fuel, energize and strengthen the pictures of your

future. This develops your faith. Discuss the miracle that is en route to you with everyone. Work on your *expectation.* Obedience is always rewarded. Everything God has promised you will come to pass. "...all these blessings shall come on thee, and overtake thee, if thou shalt hearken unto the voice of the Lord thy God," (Deuteronomy 28:2). Your life lived holy produces results. "...no good thing will he withhold from them that walk uprightly," (Psalm 84:11).

You are not fighting your battle alone. "I will be an enemy unto thine enemies, and an adversary unto thy adversaries," (Exodus 23:22).

Refuse access to yourself with anyone not in agreement with The Word of God. When satan wants to destroy you, he sends a person into your life. "Be not deceived: evil communications corrupt good manners," (1 Corinthians 15:33).

Avoid broken focus. *When the wrong people talk to you, you make the wrong decisions.*

When you make a mistake, consider yourself that much closer to your Harvest. "The Lord upholdeth all that fall, and raiseth up all those that be bowed down," (Psalm 145:14). Do not be too hard on yourself. The rewards of change are coming. Patience works.

Overcoming involves more than one battle. It is the individual who refuses to quit that wins. Always.

Never consider quitting. Never. Get up and try again. And, again. And, again. Hell fears a fighter. "Blessed is the man that endureth temptation: for when he is tried, he shall receive the crown of life which the Lord hath promised to them that love Him," (James 1:12).

My greatest blessings often come after my longest

waiting.

Several years ago, I was preaching for a friend of mine in Columbus, Ohio. At the end of the service, The Holy Spirit spoke to me to receive an offering for the pastor instead of my own ministry. Well, I desperately needed a miracle. I needed finances badly for a special project I was facing. So, any Seed I planted would be a Crisis Seed. (Remember that a Crisis Seed increases in its influence with God.) *It is possible that a small Seed sown during a crisis produces a greater Harvest than a generous Seed during good times.*

So, I agreed to give the offering in its entirety to the pastor. Then The Holy Spirit made an unusual suggestion. I really did not feel that it was a command but rather an *invitation to an investment.* I had just received a royalty check for $8,500. Actually, it was everything that I had to my name. I do not recall any money in my savings account other than this check I had in my briefcase.

"How would you like to *explore and experiment* with what I could do with your $8,500?" The Holy Spirit spoke.

It brought a moment of torment and torture. Then, I just quietly spoke in my spirit back to Him, "That's all right. I really appreciate this wonderful $8,500! It is enough Harvest for me."

He spoke the *second* time. Oh, how thankful I am for the second chances He gives to us to try again, reach again and plant again.

"How would you like to explore and experiment with what I could do with your $8,500?"

Something in me took a careful evaluation. What could I really do with $8,500? It certainly was not enough to pay my house off. What could I do? Buy a small car, or put a down payment on a rent house, or fly to Europe and vacation for a month?

I decided to believe His Word.

That decision changed my lifetime income forever. Six weeks later, God gave me an idea that brought me hundreds of thousands of dollars in return. In fact, every 90 days I still receive a royalty check for that idea.

Now, here is the powerful principle about waiting that you must grasp:

It was over *two years* after I sowed the $8,500 that I received my first nickel of profit. I went through several battles and difficulties. I thought the idea would never get off the ground. But, it did. My *willingness to wait* through 8 seasons of Harvest was worth every single hour of waiting.

Some want to plant on Sunday morning in church and reap Monday morning on their job. That is not even logical, Scriptural or promised by God. "...but he that endureth unto the end shall be saved," (Matthew 10:22).

Keep feeding your faith during the painful season of waiting. "...faith cometh by hearing and hearing by the word of God," (Romans 10:17).

Your seasons of waiting are not seasons of inactivity. Much is going on. Angels are positioning to minister. Demons are being confronted. Strategies are being developed. God is moving people into your life just like a Boaz was moved into the life of Ruth. Never believe that a season of waiting is a season of doing nothing. *The opposite is true.*

Seasons of waiting are the busiest seasons ever in

the spirit world.

Remind yourself that joy still flows in the heat of battle. "And you became followers of us, and of the Lord, having received the word in much affliction, with joy of the Holy Ghost," (1 Thessalonians 1:6).

Do not permit your ship of financial blessing to be dashed on the Rock of Impatience. Thousands have not received their financial Harvest because they got in a hurry, unwilling to trust the Lord of the Harvest. "But they that wait upon the Lord shall renew their strength; they shall mount up with wings as eagles; they shall run, and not be weary; and they shall walk and not faint," (Isaiah 40:31).

Wait Long Enough For Your Seed To Produce Your Desired Harvest.

⇜ 24 ⇝

BE WILLING TO BEGIN YOUR HARVEST WITH A SMALL SEED

Acorns Can Become Oak Trees.

But, most people keep waiting for their "ship to come in" before they begin the sowing cycle. You must *start with what you have.*

This Principle of Beginning is powerful. Every long journey starts with the first small step. Millionaires started with their first nickel. Great companies have humble beginnings. *You can go anywhere you want to go...if you are willing to take enough small steps.*

Look at the late Mary Kay Ash. She had just a few thousand dollars and a couple of shelves of products. But, she started her business. She focused on her future. At her death, she was worth over $300 million, and her business was worth $2 billion.

Look at McDonald's hamburger chain. From a humble beginning, it has become the most powerful hamburger chain on the earth. It started with a little hamburger that became popular in a town.

If you keep holding on to the Seed you have today, it will never become a Harvest. You must be willing to start your Harvest with *whatever God has already placed in your hand.* I sat in a banquet many years ago frustrated. The speaker stirred me. I desperately wanted to plant a $1,000 Seed into his ministry. I had

$10 in my pocket. "Lord, I really wish I could bless him with a $1,000 check," I whispered to the Lord.

"You have $10 in your pocket. Plant it."

"Oh, I need my $10 tonight. But, if You would give me $1,000, I promise to sow it," was my answer.

My mind started churning. How could I get more money to sow? I thought about my little office. It was in my tiny garage in Houston, Texas. That is where I studied, prayed, and also where I had a row of shelves that contained the only product I had in my ministry—one long-play album. Five hundred of those albums were on the shelves. That was approximately 6 to 8 months of sales. Then it hit me. *"Start with what you already have."*

Little hinges can swing huge doors. I could give him those 500 albums. If he sold them for $6.00 each, he would make $3,000 for his ministry. I made the decision. "Brother, I wish I had a lot to give you. I wanted to be able to write a check for $1,000, but my ministry is just beginning. I do have 500 record albums. If you would receive them from me, you can have them for selling in your crusades. If you sell them for $1 each, it would be a $500 Seed. If you sell them for $6, you would have $3,000 for your ministry." (I thought I had to explain it!)

Twelve months passed. One day, while sitting in Nairobi, Kenya, at a missionary's home, the mail came. It was a scribbled hand-written note from a major television minister, "Mike, I heard your record album. I want to purchase 40,000 of them to sell through my television program. Please rush me 40,000 albums. I will send you a check for them next week." I shouted all over that room.

The profit enabled me to purchase a beautiful Lincoln Town Car for cash! It launched a different season for my ministry. I was on air every time I drove up to a church for a crusade. Why? *I started with whatever was already in my hand.*

Last week, a lady wrote me a check for $5. She was embarrassed. She said, "I'm so ashamed to send you such a small check, but it's all that I have." I was reading her letter about 2:00 in the morning after coming in from a major meeting. My heart was so stirred. You see, what she was planting was *enough to impress God.*

He knows how *much* you have.

He knows how *little* you have.

Your obedience secures His attention.

You don't have to write God a huge check for $100,000 to move His hand toward you. You simply have to obey the inner voice of The Holy Spirit with *whatever you presently possess.*

Remember the incredible picture of the widow? "And Jesus sat over against the treasury, and beheld how the people cast money into the treasury: and many that were rich cast in much. And there came a certain poor widow, and she threw in two mites, which make a farthing. And He called unto Him His disciples, and saith unto them, Verily I say unto you, That this poor widow hath cast more in, than all they which have cast into the treasury: For all they did cast in of their abundance; but she of her want did cast in all that she had, even all her living," (Mark 12:41-44).

She started her Harvest with what she had.

I have sown jewelry, cars, clothes into other lives. I have planted hundreds of thousands of books and tapes as special Seeds. You see, everything you have is a Seed.

If you keep it today, that is your Harvest. But if you release it, it becomes a Seed.

What you presently possess is only a Seed if you sow it into soil. When you keep it in your hand, it becomes the only Harvest you will ever have. Look around you. Is there a piece of furniture that a widow needs at her house? Could you volunteer two hours a week at your home church? That is a Seed.

Start with what you have.

You are a Walking Warehouse of Seeds. You have more inside you than you could ever imagine. But, you must take the time to inventory *everything* God has given you. Do not permit pride to rob you of an opportunity to plant a Seed. When the offering plate is passed, even if you only possess $2.00 in your pocket—plant it.

Get your Harvest started.

As a parent, teach your child the importance of sowing something *consistently* in the work of God. It may only be a dime or a quarter. But, you will create a flow and river of Harvest that will outlast every attack against your life.

Millions are waiting for more. They refuse to start their Harvest with a small Seed. It is one of the reasons they will never receive everything God wants to send to them. "Though thy beginning was small, yet thy latter end should greatly increase," (Job 8:7).

What you have will create anything else you *want—if you sow it.*

⇜ 25 ⇝

QUALIFY THE SOIL

The Quality of The Soil Affects The Growing of The Seed.

That is why Jesus never invested time in persuading Pharisees. He was the Son of God. He knew it. It was *their* responsibility to *discern* it. He knew they were "fools and blind," (Matthew 23:17).

Yet, He took time to go home with the tax collector, Zacchaeus. You see, He discerned soil *worthy* of His attention and time.

Two thieves were crucified besides Christ. One received mercy. One did not. Why? The thief who believed in the Divinity of Jesus reached out. Jesus responded. *Both* thieves had needs. *Both* needed the miracle of salvation. But, Jesus took the time to respond to the one who reached out. He was *the good soil.*

Jesus taught the importance of observing the *quality of the soil.* "Hearken; Behold, there went out a sower to sow: And it came to pass, as he sowed, some fell by the way side, and the fowls of the air came and devoured it up. And some fell on stony ground where it had not much earth; and immediately it sprang up, because it had no depth of earth: But when the sun was up, it was scorched; and because it had no root, it withered away. And some fell among thorns, and the thorns grew up and choked it and it yielded no fruit.

And other fell on good ground, and did yield fruit that sprang up and increased; and brought forth, some thirty, and some sixty, and some an hundred," (Mark 4:3-8).

Refuse to sow Seed into the life of a non-giver. Suppose you have a son-in-law that needs financial help. What do you do? Do you hand him money? Or, do you provide him an *opportunity* to *earn* it? There is a great difference. A lady approached me one night after a meeting and discussed her plight with me. Her son-in-law and daughter had been staying with her for several weeks.

"I feel so sorry for them. They are out of jobs. They need money. They are really going through a great financial trial at this time," she said tearfully.

"So, what does he do everyday at your home?"

"Well, they usually sleep in until 10:00 or so. Then, they watch television. They are waiting for doors to open," she explained.

"Does your daughter prepare your food while you are at work every day?" I asked.

"Oh no. She does not like to cook!"

"Does your son-in-law wash your dishes, clean your house or has he waxed your car, mowed the grass while you are gone to work these days?"

"Well, he's kind of depressed right now. He really does not feel like working. And, I hate to ask him anyway," was her reply.

I showed her in Scripture the commandments that Paul wrote to the church at Thessalonica. "For even when we were with you, this we commanded you, that if any would not work, neither should he eat," (2 Thessalonians 3:10). He called those who did not work "disorderly," (verse 11).

The Apostle Paul instructed us to avoid having any fellowship or friendship with those who refuse to be productive. "And if any man obey not our word by this epistle, note that man, and have no company with him, that he may be ashamed," (2 Thessalonians 3:14).

Now, a lazy person is not necessarily your enemy. But, his unproductivity is to be noted, confronted, addressed and penalized. (See 2 Thessalonians 3:15.)

They are unproductive soil.

Refuse to sow Seed into a church that is against financial blessing. Why would I support any ministry that is in direct rebellion to the Laws of Provision according to Scripture?

"Well, Mike, I am out of work."

"Well, you might want to define that a little differently, since God has only promised to 'bless all the work of thine hand,'" (Deuteronomy 28:12). You see, you can *find* work. Anybody can *find some kind of work.* It may not pay $40 an hour at first. It may not be the easiest thing you've ever done. But, work is everywhere you look in life.

Refuse to sow Seed in someone who is unteachable.

"I really need help. We cannot pay our bills. Can you help us at this time?" one of my relatives asked me rather boldly one day.

"Let's sit down. I want to review your finances with you," I replied. "Give me a list of what you owe. Show me what you are doing to earn money. I'm going to give you some advice, and if you'll follow this advice, I will consider investing in you."

He said he did not have the time! Think about it. He did not have enough desire to prosper to even provide me a list of his bills and enter into a counseling session with me. He was unqualified to receive any Seed. *That is bad soil.* "Poverty and shame shall be to him that refuseth instruction: but he that regardeth reproof shall be honoured," (Proverbs 13:18).

Look for good soil continually. Now, there are many people near you that are good soil. Hundreds of ministries deserve our best Seed-sowing. Look around you. Evaluate. Observe those who are productive around you. Boaz did this when he saw Ruth. He instructed servants to make it easier for her to secure a Harvest, "handfuls of purpose."

I love to sow Seed in young ministers. You see, they are emptying their lives into the gospel. Some have left good jobs and promise of fortune to help broken lives become healed. They do not have the rewards of momentum, great reputations established yet. I believe this produces great fruit.

I love to send money to ministers who are spreading this gospel of provision. I know their warfare. They are despised by the world, misunderstood by the church, and fought by those who do not understand the message of prosperity. So, I want to provide them Seed to keep this message of supernatural Harvest accessible.

I love to sow Seed in proven ministries. They have fought a good fight. They have kept the faith. They have endured. *Endurance should be honored.*

"Mike, every time I plant a Seed in your ministry something wonderful happens in my ministry," a minister explained recently. Well, I really appreciated his statement, but I felt a little embarrassed. He continued. "Mike, there really is a difference when I sow Seed in *good soil.* It seems that my Harvest comes quickly, with great excellence and I feel at peace about my Seed-sowing."

Sow Seed into those *who have helped you.*

Sow Seed into *those who have given you wise counsel and correction.*

Sow Seed into the lives of those who stayed *loyal and faithful.*

Sow Seed into those who are *willing to labor, toil and empty their life out for the cause of the gospel.* "And let us not be weary in well doing: for in due season we shall reap, if we faint not," (Galatians 6:9).

Many are not choosing the soil carefully where they sow their Seed. That is one of the reasons they will never reap the hundredfold return God would like for them to experience.

Our Prayer Together...

"Father, where should I be sowing? Reveal the soil that will produce. Show me...I will not waste any Seed on unproductive soil. In Jesus' name. Amen."

❧ 1 Corinthians 16:2 ❧

"Upon the first day of the week let every one of you lay by him in store, as God hath prospered him, that there be no gatherings when I come."

❧ 26 ❧

SOW CONSISTENTLY

When You Sow Continuously, Your Harvest Will Become Continuous.

When you sow inconsistently, your Harvest will become erratic. Many years ago I talked to a young couple after service. They were distraught. Discouraged. Blaming God for everything that happened in their life. When I approached the subject of tithing and sowing, they both jumped in with indignation.

"We have tried that already. It did not work for us."

It is a dangerous thing to call God a liar.

It shows a lack of the fear of God.

It reveals pride and arrogance. When you deliberately tell others that you have obeyed the Scriptures, and God's word did not work for you, it is a dangerous and fearful thing.

"I would like to see your check stubs sometime," I countered. "I would like to see the *consistency* of your tithing. This is very important. If you have tithed and sowed Seed continuously for several months, through several seasons, this needs to be validated. Because the God I serve is not a liar. He said He would open the windows of Heaven upon you. So, if you have missed any weeks of tithing, your Harvest will become erratic and unpredictable."

They stuttered around. Then, they admitted that they had only "tried tithing" a few times. It was not a routine and pattern of their life. It was not their lifestyle.

Observe the seasons. They are predictable winter, spring, summer and fall create such regularity that we build our lives on the laws of this earth.

I sat in a remarkable seminar many years ago in Madrid, Spain. The scientist was explaining the distance and complications involved in landing a rocket on the moon. He stated that landing a rocket on the moon required such precision that it was the equivalent of a man *shooting a mosquito 68 miles away with a rifle.* Someone asked how would it be possible to do such a thing?

"Laws. This entire universe has specific laws that can be discovered when you cooperate with the Laws of the Universe. You can predict exactly where a rocket can be sent," he explained.

The ancient writer made it so clear, "To every thing there is a season, and a time to every purpose under the Heaven: A time to be born, and a time to die; a time to plant, and a time to pluck up that which is planted...A time to get, and a time to lose; a time to keep, and a time to cast away," (read Ecclesiastes 3:1-8).

You must learn the power of rhythm, routine and consistency. It is important to establish this in your sowing and reaping. Acknowledge that your life is an endless and continuous cycle of sowing and reaping, giving and receiving. Work with it. Do not work against it. Nature has a pattern. You can oppose it, hate it and despise it. But, the only way to reap the benefits and rewards is to observe and to cooperate with it.

Create a personal schedule for sowing Seeds into God's work. The Apostle Paul understood this principle. "Now concerning the collection for the saints, as I have given order to the churches of Galatia, even so do ye. *Upon the first day of the week* let every one of you lay by him in store as God hath prospered him, that there be no gatherings when I come," (1 Corinthians 16:1-2).

Reaping does not follow sowing.

Waiting follows sowing.

You sow. You wait. You reap.

So, for you to experience a continuous incoming Harvest, there must be a *continuous sowing of Seed* to accommodate the seasons of waiting. As long as earth exists, seasons will exist. "While the earth remaineth, seedtime and harvest, and cold and heat, and summer and winter, and day and night shall not cease," (Genesis 8:22).

4 Reasons People Refuse To Sow Consistently

1. Some Refuse To Sow Consistently Because Their Faith And Confidence In God Wavers. When they listen to a man of God with a specific anointing, they become responsive. As they sit under that anointing, faith comes alive within them. They get excited. Their faith is vibrant. Their confidence in God is renewed. Faith requires action. *It is almost impossible to sit under a man of God who unlocks the flow of faith and not plant a Seed.* In fact, it is a dangerous and tragic condition if you ever come to the place where you can set under that kind of anointing and close your heart to it. So, it is only natural to become responsive to the *call of faith within you.* Some sneer at this. They have contempt and belittle this.

They call it "emotional giving."

I don't quite understand them. If God puts a faith in your heart to plant a Seed, it is His nature rising up strong within you.

That desire to give *cannot be satanic.*

That desire to give *cannot be human.*

The desire to give is *the nature of God Himself.*

Some, a few days after they have been in the presence of God and His anointing, enter into conversations with those who lack faith. Critics. Scorners. The fearful.

"You were crazy to give an offering to that preacher. Don't you realize he will just buy a nice car and fancy clothes with your tithe and offering?" snears the ungodly person at the faith-filled believer.

This kind of statement poisons their mind. Their heart becomes confused. Spiritual frustration sets in. You will leave the Arena of Faith and enter into the *sewage of human debate.*

It is the quickest way to lose your Harvest. You see, your Harvest requires faith, not merely a Seed.

Your Seed is *what* you sow.

Your faith is *why* He multiplies it.

God responds to your Seed *because it is wrapped with faith.* He wants to be believed. He responds to faith *anywhere He finds it.* Even a sinner will get a miracle *when he believes.* This happened continuously in the Kathryn Kuhlman meetings. I have watched people get miracle after miracle. She would ask, "Are you a Christian?"

"No," came the hesitant replies.

Why would God heal a sinner? *Faith.* "...faith was reckoned to Abraham for righteousness," (Romans 4:9). "The word is nigh thee, even in thy mouth, and in thine heart: that is, the word of faith, which we preach," (Romans 10:8).

So, don't expect an unsaved, rebellious and ungodly loved one to be excited when you plant a Seed into the work of God. They do not even appreciate Calvary yet. Jesus is unimportant to them. They sneer at the Scriptures. They are entangled in the tentacles of hell, like an octopus. They can purchase their liquor, cigarettes and gamble in the Casinos. But, when they find out their widowed mother gave money to a preacher, their fury will erupt like a volcano.

Refuse their intimidation and scorn.

The opinions of your friends will influence you, so be careful. It matters. This is normal. However, do not expect someone unresponsive to The Holy Spirit, rebellious toward the principles of The Word of God to understand your sowing Seeds to spread this glorious gospel.

Doubt is not the only reason we refuse to sow with regularity. I have known of many people who get angry at a preacher and *hold their tithe back.*

"When my pastor does something to upset me, I simply stop paying tithe," one lady said with fervor and anger. "God understands!"

You better know He understands. He understands your scorn, ingratitude and immaturity. You have not hurt your pastor when you withhold the tithe. You have not stopped the militant and victorious march of the church toward victory by withholding your tithe.

You have destroyed the supply line for your own family. You have created seasons of devastation in your future. You have played the part of a fool. Satan fed you a lie. He baited the hook and like an ignorant fish, you fell for it.

2.   Some Stop Sowing Consistently Because They Want To Use The Money For Something Special They Want To Purchase. They intend to pay it back. The car payment comes due. They see a refrigerator they want to buy. So, they talk themselves into *using the tithe* that week for personal use. *It is the quickest way to financial suicide.*

You cannot afford to *touch* what belongs to God.

You cannot afford to *keep* what belongs to God.

It is a lie from satan designed to maneuver you to a place of financial wipe out and devastation. Satan hates and despises you. He despises the flow of blessing in your life. That is why He was so angry about the blessings of Job.

Anything God *loves* is something satan *hates.* Anything God *blesses* is something satan *curses.*

3.   Others Do Not Sow With Regularity Simply Because They Give As They Are Feeling It. If I only gave when I felt it, I would not give very often. You see, my own needs often overwhelm me. When I look at a stack of television and radio bills, I can easily lose the "feeling" to go bless the work of God. In fact, I just saw an estimate to repair my roof. My house has been leaking for several weeks, and I have been too busy to get it repaired. (Or, maybe I just don't want to pay for it!) At any rate, as I look at the incredible cost of a new roof on my flat topped house, I lose every feeling and desire to write a check for the work of God. It is the last thing I "feel like doing." You cannot afford to sow as you are *feeling* it.

You must focus on regularity. "In the morning sow thy Seed, and in the evening withhold not thine hand: for thou knowest not whether shall prosper, either this or that, or whether they both shall be alike good," (Ecclesiastes 11:6). *Learn to sow into many ministries, not just one.* "Give generously, for your gifts will return to you later. Divide your gifts among many, for in the days ahead you yourself may need much help," (Ecclesiastes 11:1-2, Living Bible).

I like the King James version of this too. "Cast thy bread upon the waters: for thou shalt find it after many days. Give a portion to seven, and also to eight; for thou knowest not what evil shall be upon the earth," (Ecclesiastes 11:1-2).

4. Some Do Not Sow With Regularity Because They Are In Continuous Crisis. When crisis comes, they quit giving. When blessing occurs, then they sow. If you sow according to your circumstances only, you will sow *inconsistently.* "He that observeth the wind shall not sow; and he that regardeth the clouds shall not reap," (Ecclesiastes 11:4).

Millions will stay in poverty because they refuse to enter the Miracle of *Consistent* Sowing.

RECOMMENDED INVESTMENTS:
Creating Tomorrow Through Seed-Faith (Book/B-06/32 pgs)
Seeds of Wisdom on Seed-Faith (Book/B-16/32 pgs)
My Seed Testimony (Book/B-242/32 pgs)

≈ 2 Corinthians 9:6 ≈

"He which soweth sparingly shall reap also
sparingly; and he which soweth bountifully
shall reap also bountifully."

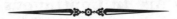

≈ 27 ≈

SOW PROPORTIONATE TO THE HARVEST YOU DESIRE

The Size of Your Seed Determines The Size of Your Harvest.

The Apostle Paul made this clear, "He which soweth sparingly shall reap also sparingly; and he which soweth bountifully shall reap also bountifully," (2 Corinthians 9:6).

I will never forget an experience in the Northeast. A large lady moved toward me after service.

"I'm believing God to make me a millionaire. And, I believe it will happen within 12 months. Here's my Seed to make it happen." She thrust something into my hand. I looked at her and said, "I am believing God with you."

After she walked away, I opened my hand. It was a crumpled dollar bill. *A dollar bill.*

Now there is nothing wrong with sowing a small Seed. *Everything must have a beginning point.* Jesus commended the woman who gave a small offering— because *it was all she had.* He said that she gave more than anyone else present that day.

But, Jesus did not say that her small offering was necessarily going to make her a *millionaire.* You see, your Seed must be comparable to the Harvest you are sowing toward.

You cannot plant a Chevrolet Seed and produce a Rolls Royce Harvest. This was what Paul was teaching. If you sow small, you will still reap. But, it will not be a large Harvest. *It will be proportionate to your Seed.* (Read 2 Corinthians 9:6.) Millions have not grasped this. They continue to roll up dollar bills, drop them in the offering plate, and hope no one watches. Yet, they are writing their prayer requests as if they are expecting Cadillacs, yachts and million dollar homes.

You can *begin* with a small Seed. When God begins to bless that small Seed, *you must increase the size of the Seed if you want the Harvest to increase.*

Let me give you an example. If you come to me and say, "Mike, I really need a house. My family is growing. I have 3 children. Right now, my wife and 3 children are living in a small two bedroom apartment. It is almost unbearable. We do not even have a refrigerator, nor a car. What should I do?"

First, I will not tell you to plant a $5 Seed toward your $100,000 home you are wanting. I would encourage you to work with the various levels of faith in front of you. *A step at a time.*

Obviously, you have not been operating with great faith or you would not be in this kind of situation.

Your faith has been *low.*

Your Seeds have *not* been planted.

Or, patience is a needed ingredient for this season.

"What is the best Seed you can sow at this time? What kind of faith is operating in you today?" I ask.

"Oh, I have $50 that I want to plant!" you answer.

I would reply, "Wonderful. Now, let's focus this Seed for an automobile comparable to this Seed. Do not ask for a $20,000 automobile from a $50 Seed. That is

4 times the promised hundredfold of Mark 10:28-30. Obviously, you're not accustomed to planting Seed, using your faith, nor even working with the laws of patience and expectation.

"Ask God for something you cannot doubt. Then, plant a Seed comparable to the Harvest you have pure faith toward. You must separate your wishes from your faith. You must separate your fantasy from your faith."

Now, many do not understand the *Principle of Progress.* Line upon line. Precept upon precept. Here a little and there a little. There is a season of "growing up" in your Christian life.

It is the same principle in the financial arena of your life. Why is this so important? When you sow a $2 Seed toward something that is out of balance, you will become disappointed, discouraged and disillusioned. You will become angry at God. You will say, "I planted a Seed and this did not multiply!"

Maybe it *is* multiplying. Maybe, the $100 bill you have in your purse was produced by the $2 Seed. But, you are not noticing it because you wanted a $20,000 Harvest.

You must learn to move from glory to glory.

I told about an incredible miracle in my life one night. I was sitting in a beautiful Mustang convertible. Teal bottom and white top. Gorgeous. It had "fun" written all over the car!

"I just bought this car this week," my friend explained. "However, I decided that I want a jeep instead. Do you think you might want to buy this car from me?"

"I think I may!" was my reply.

The next day, we pulled up at a service station.

After he filled the tank, he went inside to pay the bill. I began to pray in the Spirit. Suddenly, I began to feel *a faith rise up in me* for him to sow this as a Seed into my life. Now, that sounds a little crazy. But, I began to pray intensely. When he got back in the car, he looked at me. He cocked his head sideways and said, "You really like this car?"

"I *love* this car," I gushed.

"Your ministry has so affected and blessed me, I have been wondering what I could do to bless you." He handed me the keys with a smile. The car was mine. *Free.* An incredible gift that will stay in my heart forever.

So, when I was in a crusade later, I shared this story. I told everyone that I was going to pray that the *mantle of favor* would come upon their life. I explained that *one day of favor was worth a thousand days of labor.* When God wants to bless you, He puts somebody close to you who cares about your life and needs.

A young man approached me after church a little disgruntled. Agitated. Frustrated.

"I did that already and it did not work," he explained. "I planted a Seed several months ago and I have never had a car given to me. I need transportation. Why didn't it work for me?"

"Have you ever *planted* a car in the life of someone else?" I asked.

"No, I have not," was his hesitant and reluctant reply.

"*I have.* That's why my faith worked for me. I had already planted a car and I had every right and ability to expect one to be *given back to me*," I explained.

You cannot expect faith toward your life what you

have not faithed away from your life...

You will only have the faith to call in toward your life something that you have sown out.

Now, there are wonderful moments of mercy and grace where God will let you have something that you have been given—money or whatever, a piece of jewelry or whatever—and He will use that as a picture of your faith for a different kind of Harvest. I have seen that happen many, many times. But, your faith works *the most, the strongest,* when you have planted a Seed comparable to the Harvest you would desire.

When you are willing to work with the different levels of your faith and sow Seed proportionately, you will be amazed at the changes that will happen in your financial prosperity.

✍ 2 Chronicles 20:20 ✍

"Believe in the Lord your God, so shall ye be
established; believe His prophets, so shall
ye prosper."

⚮ 28 ⚮

Never Rebel Against An Instruction From A Financial Deliverer God Has Anointed To Unlock Your Faith

Faith Moments Are Miracle Moments.

Observe Elijah. He looked into the anguished face of a tormented widow of Zarephath. Can you possibly imagine the depths of sorrow to which her soul had plunged? She had watched her emaciated son wither and swivel up before her very eyes. She had taken a long, slow march to a tragedy. Her problem was not a mere broken down automobile. Her problem was not making her house note on time. Her financial dream was not some "new clothes."

She had one meal between her and death.

Is this the kind of crisis that inspires *giving?* Hardly. It is the kind of moment that inspires *hoarding.* You are angry. You are sad. You are hurting. You do not want to hear any preacher discuss "sowing Seed." In fact, any talk about offerings would infuriate and anger a person in this kind of crisis. It would be normal for her to say to Elijah, "If you had the heart of God, you would be giving to the poor instead of asking for money from me. If you really knew God, you would have brought me a meal, instead of an offering envelope."

She had every reason to question his validity as a man of God. Where was his sensitivity? Where was his compassion, the proof he cared?

The proof that he cared was his refusal to bog down and wallow with her in sympathy and self-pity. He fueled her faith, not her self-pity. She had every reason to question him, but, she did not. She had something that few *have—the ability to recognize a man of God when he came along.* She had the ability to listen to a challenge instead of criticize it.

When God Loves You Enough To Assign A Man of God To Unlock Your Faith, You Must Recognize It As The Moment For Your Miracle.

I had a puzzling and troubling experience several years ago. It was at one of my World Wisdom Conferences. I will never forget it as long as I live. Someone handed me a note and said, "A minister here feels led to receive an offering for your ministry."

"No, I have already received one. This is not the time," I replied. One of my closest friends, Nancy Harmon, came and stood beside me and whispered.

"Mike, this man really wants to receive an offering. He feels that God has spoken to him specifically at this point to receive an offering."

"No, Nancy. I'm the host here, and I really do not feel God in this at all."

Within a few moments, our evangelist friend came to me. Tears are in his eyes and on his face. He is shaking his head. "Brother, I'm supposed to receive an offering for your ministry."

It bothered me. It almost agitated and angered me. Nobody wants to be led by The Holy Spirit more than Mike Murdock. I am more sensitive than anybody could imagine. (Anyone who has written over 5,000 songs is sensitive!) I simply never felt the "wind of God" blowing in *that service* for finances. *I had a different plan* for an offering later that night. I had already received an offering earlier.

But, I could not doubt he was a man of God.

His life proved it. *Proven* men of God embraced him as a credible evangelist. Thousands had come to Christ through him. He was dynamic. Articulate. He obviously carried the Mantle of financial blessing upon his life.

So, I gave him the microphone. I felt as cold as Alaska, but stood quietly nearby. He cried. Everybody else cried. The offering was received. Many people rushed to the front. They were carrying checks for $1,000 and many others came for faith-promises. *I never did feel God in it.* Even to this day, as I remember those moments, I never "felt" God in the entire offering. However, every one else received incredible blessing and happiness. Testimonies have come from the service. Over $100,000 was promised or given to our ministry to buy television time. *Yet, I stood in the presence of the man of God and did not feel anything.*

But, God *required* me to trust His man, whether I felt it or not. Had I refused to trust the challenge of a man of God, my partners would have lost all their Harvests. My ministry would have lost $100,000 to purchase television air time. Bills would have been unpaid. Oh, I wonder how much has been lost through our *unwillingness to accept the man God sends to us?*

If you could see how much financial blessing has been lost because of the moments you decided to go by your feelings, it would sicken your heart. If God were to replay the voice of every man of God He had sent to you, and show you your response, you would not be able to sleep tonight.

Your heart would be broken.

I was in Tulsa during the month of June, 1994. After a board meeting, I went into a major service. A wonderful minister friend of mine took the microphone and proceeded to receive an offering. I had already given this ministry several thousand dollars. So, I sat calmly as others prepared their offerings. My checkbook was at home (I don't like to give cash). I had no intention of giving whatsoever. Suddenly, he said, "I want every ministry here to plant a Seed of $200." If I remember correctly, he told us to focus for a double portion of the presence of God, and a real visitation of The Holy Spirit in our lives. Of course, nothing was even implied that you could buy a *miracle* from God. Any fool knows you cannot buy a miracle from God. Certainly you cannot *buy* The Holy Spirit.

Suddenly my minister friend announced, "While The Holy Spirit is hovering over this place, *while the soil is moist,* plant your Seed. Do it *now.*"

I had no interest in sowing another Seed. None. I give and give and give. Sometimes, I am simply tired of giving. Especially to a ministry that has received so much from me already.

Now, I have a fear of God in my life. It operates strongly. The thought of "missing the will of God" is terrifying to me.

Something touched *my spirit.* I knew it was *important* for me to plant this Seed of $200. I reached inside, reluctantly, but *obediently*, and pulled out two $100 bills. I sowed the Seed. And, walked out of the conference and never thought about my Seed again.

But, The Holy Spirit remembered.

Oh, I am so thankful for The precious Holy Spirit in my life! He has salvaged me from so many crises! He has opened so many Golden Doors of Opportunity! He has created the Golden Connection with so many precious friends! He is our precious Source of Blessing!

My Harvest came in less than 30 days.

I went to bed at 5:00 a.m. on a Wednesday morning, July 13, 1994. Two hours later, I was awakened by The Holy Spirit. That was the greatest day in my lifetime of memories. I had an indescribable, unforgettable encounter with The Holy Spirit on July 13. I would trade every other discovery of my lifetime for what I had discovered about The Holy Spirit on that day. *Less than 30 days after my Seed of $200...in obedience to a man of God.* Since then, I have written hundreds of songs to The Holy Spirit, held scores of Schools of The Holy Spirit and watched thousands enter into the greatest season of their spiritual life. The answer was simple.

I obeyed an instruction of a man of God.

At some point in your life, God will place His servant in front of you. His servant will look you in the eye and challenge you to plant a Seed of obedience.

It will be an *illogical* Seed. It will be a *challenging* Seed. A Seed of faith.

It will require every ounce of your faith.

If you choose to reject this challenge, you will abort the most glorious Season of Harvest you could have ever tasted.

If you choose to obey the man of God, the Golden Door of Blessing will swing wide and you will *step out of famine* into the Season of Prosperity you have desired your entire life.

You are not forgotten by God.

Nobody loves you more than the Person who created you. Your fears are known by Him. Your tears matter to Him. When you are hurting, He is bringing answers toward you. Every moment of your life God schedules miracles like currents of blessing into your life.

Every prison will have a *door.*

Every river will have a *bridge.*

Every mountain will have a *tunnel.*

But, you must *find* it. Look for it. Listen for it. Search for it. Believe that it exists. "There hath no temptation taken you but such as is common to man: but God is faithful, who will not suffer you to be tempted above that ye are able; but will with the temptation also make a way to escape, that ye may be able to bear it," (1 Corinthians 10:13).

You must pursue those God is using to fuel your faith. There are wonderful men and women of God who carry financial anointings. They can unlock your faith. It may involve a 4-hour drive to their crusade. *But it is important that you honor and treasure and pursue their mantle.* Listen to their tapes. Read their books. Listen to their heart.

They have tasted failure. They *know how to get out of trouble.* They know what sleepless nights are like. They have fought the demons of fear and uncertainty.

That is why they are qualified to mentor you.

Some will never taste their financial Harvest because they are sitting under leaders *who fuel their doubts and unbelief.* They listen to relatives who continuously discuss the economic problems on the earth, hard times and how difficult life is.

The voices you keep listening to are the voices you will eventually believe.

Ten spies infected millions of the Israelites with their unbelief and doubt. When they talked about the giants, the people forgot about the grapes of blessing.

Whatever You Talk About Will Increase.

What you think about becomes larger.

Your mind and your mouth are magnifiers of anything you want to *grow*.

Two spies came back with faith, victory and the ability to overcome giants. Their names were Joshua and Caleb. These had been with God. They had seen the giants, but were not afraid. They had seen the grapes and decided to become champions. They had experienced too many days in the wilderness to be satisfied with failure.

They became the champions of faith. Joshua became the leader after the death of Moses. Caleb became known for "taking his mountain." Oh, the rewards of faith are sweet. The taste of victory stays in your mouth so long!

You must discern the Joshua and Caleb nearest you. Find the faith food. Listen for faith talk. Sit under it and listen and absorb. *Something within you will grow.*

I receive much inspiration from the story of Elijah and the widow in 1 Kings 17. I never tire of this incredible Well of Wisdom. The widow was hurting. Devastated. Starving. She was one meal from death.

That is when a man of faith was sent into her life.

He did not criticize her, coddle her or sympathize

with her. He knew *how* to get her *out of trouble.*

She had to listen to him. She had to discern that he was a man of God. She had to be willing to follow his instructions, regardless of how ridiculous and illogical they appeared to her natural mind.

A man of God often holds the Golden Key to your financial deliverance. If you respect that anointing, the chains will fall off. Blindness will disappear. Your eyes will behold the Golden Path to blessing. If you become critical, resentful and rebellious, you will forfeit the most remarkable season of miracles God has ever scheduled into your life.

Nobody can discern a man of God for you. *You* must do it. Nobody can force you to obey a man of God. Your heart must be soft and broken before God, enough to follow.

You may only receive one opportunity to obey the instruction that brings your deliverance. (Nabal only received one opportunity to feed and bless the army of David.)

You must recognize greatness when you are in the presence of it. It will not always demand attention. Jesus was many places where He was undiscerned, undetected and unrecognized. His own family did not recognize His mantle, His Assignment and that He was the Son of God. He did come unto His own and His own received Him not.

You may have to find the man of God before he looks for you. You see, he is *not* needing you. *You* are needing him.

Read the incredible story of Saul and his servant, who had lost their donkeys. They were so disturbed until the servant remembered that *a man of God* lived in the area. He knew the power of an offering. They both made the decision to find the Prophet Samuel. The rest of the story is absolutely incredible. When they came into the presence of Samuel, the anointing from Samuel began to flow toward them. (See 1 Samuel 9:3-10:10.)

They had brought their Seed.

They brought an offering.

They believed he was a man of God.

That encounter with Samuel catapulted Saul into the kingship of Israel.

Somewhere, there is a man of God with the Golden Key to your house of treasure. Your responsibility is to discern it, find him and obey the instruction.

Several years ago, my assistant listened to me share the miracle of the "Covenant of Blessing," the sowing of the $58 Seed. (My first encounter was in Washington, DC, when The Holy Spirit spoke to me to plant a $58 Seed to represent the 58 kinds of miracles I had found in Scripture. It launched an incredible parade of miracles in my personal life. I have told about this in hundreds of places.)

Now, my assistant was a good young man who loved God. But, something happened as he listened to me tell the story. I instructed him and others in that service to, *"Give your Seed an Assignment.* Write on the check where you want to experience the Harvest in your own personal life."

He wrote the $58 Seed, and then wrote "better family relations" on the left side of the check. Here are 7 miracles that happened after that Seed:

1. His mother came to Christ within 14 days.
2. His two sisters came to Christ within 14 days.

3.   His daughter came to Christ within 14 days.

4.   He got to spend a week with his two other daughters that he had not seen in 5 years.

5.   He was able to have a meal and afternoon with his entire family—it had not happened in the previous 15 years.

6.   His 86-year-old father came to Christ within 90 days.

7.   His oldest sister, who had run away from home 48 years prior, was located and came back home for a family reunion. (Nobody had seen nor heard from her for 48 long years. She was considered dead.)

Everyone of these miracles happened within 90 days of his sowing his Seed of $58.

Why? *He followed the instruction of a man of God.* Almost everywhere I go, I ask those who need miracles to plant a Seed. A specific Seed. Usually, I ask them to plant a Seed of $58 (sometimes it is more, depending on the instructions of The Holy Spirit). The miracles are incredible. I get letters from everywhere relating the supernatural intervention of God *following their acts of obedience.*

A woman in Knoxville, Tennessee, approached me with a tall husband by her side. "Remember that $58 Seed?" she asked.

"Yes."

"This is him! He was away from Christ and within a few days after my Seed, he came with me to church and gave his heart to God."

The man of God sent may not be packaged like you anticipated. John the Baptist had an appearance many could not tolerate. But, God was with him. His best gifts do not always arrive in silk. He often uses burlap bags to package His best prizes. Men do look on the outward appearance, while God looks on the heart.

Those God sends into your life may have harsh or uncomfortable personalities. If you could have heard Isaiah or Ezekiel, you might be shocked at some of the strong language that poured from their lips.

Those God sends with a special challenge to your faith may not appear socially fit. God often uses foolish things to confound the wise. You will not discern them through the hearing of the ear nor the seeing of the eye.

You will discern them by the Spirit of God within you.

"Believe in the Lord your God, so shall ye be established; believe His prophets, so shall ye prosper," (2 Chronicles 20:20).

When you begin to acknowledge the Word of the Lord coming from proven and established servants of God, the flow of miracles will multiply and increase toward you.

Our Prayer Together...

"Oh, Father, forgive us for staying in the arena of self-righteousness, logic and human ability. When You bring Your servant into our life, it is to bless and empower us. You inspire us to let go of something in our hand so You will let go of what is in Your hand for us. In Jesus' name. Amen."

RECOMMENDED INVESTMENTS:
31 Reasons People Do Not Receive Their Financial Harvest
  (Book/B-82/252 pgs)
31 Reasons People Do Not Receive Their Financial Harvest
  (CD/CDS-38)

≈ Numbers 23:19 ≈

"God is not a man, that He should lie."

∼ 29 ∼

ALWAYS SOW WITH THE EXPECTATION OF A RETURN

You Can Only Do What You Know.

Thousands have been taught that it is wrong to expect something in return when you give something to God. They feel that this is proof of greed.

"When I give to God, I expect nothing in return," is the prideful claim of many who have been taught this terrible error.

Do you expect a salary from your boss at the end of a work week? Of course, you do. Is this greed? Hardly.

Did you expect forgiveness when you confessed your sins to Christ? Of course, you did. Is this greed? Hardly.

Stripping expectation from your Seed is theft of the *only pleasure God knows.*

Remember, God's greatest need is to be believed. His greatest pain is to be doubted. "But without faith it is impossible to please Him: for he that cometh to God must believe that He is, and that He is a rewarder of them that diligently seek Him," (Hebrews 11:6).

Motive means *reason for doing something.*

When someone on trial is accused of a murder, they try to find the motive or reason why a person would do such a horrible thing.

God expected you to be motivated by supply, the

promise of provision. "Give, and it shall be given unto you, good measure, pressed down and shaken together, and running over, shall men give into your bosom," (Luke 6:38). (This is much more than a principle of mercy and forgiveness. This is a Principle in Supply.)

God offers overflow as a reason you should sow Seed. Seeds of forgiveness or whatever you need. "Honour the Lord with thy substance, and with the firstfruits of all thine increase: So shall thy barns be filled with plenty, and thy presses shall burst out with new wine," (Proverbs 3:9-10). Notice that He paints the picture of *overflowing barns* to motivate us (give us a reason) for honoring Him.

He promised benefits to those who might be fearful about tithing. "Bring ye all the tithes into the storehouse, that there may be meat in Mine house, and prove Me now herewith, saith the Lord of hosts, if I will not open you the windows of Heaven, and pour you out a blessing, that there shall not be room enough to receive it," (Malachi 3:10).

Read Deuteronomy 28:1-14. Here in Scripture God creates a list of the specific blessings that will occur *if you obey Him.* Why does He give us these portraits of prosperity? *To inspire you and give you a reason for obedience.*

Peter needed this kind of encouragement just like you and I do today. He felt such emptiness as he related to Christ that he and the others had "given up everything."

Jesus promised a one hundredfold return. "Then Peter began to say unto Him, Lo, we have left all, and have followed Thee. And Jesus answered and said, Verily I say unto you, There is no man that hath left house, or brethren, or sisters, or father, or mother, or wife, or children, or lands, for My sake, and the gospel's, But he shall receive an hundredfold now in this time, houses, and brethren, and sisters, and mothers, and children, and lands, with persecutions; and in the world to come eternal life," (Mark 10:28-30).

Many people think it is evil to sow for a Harvest. *That is the reason to sow.*

Giving is the cure for greed, not hoarding.

When you sow to get a Harvest, you have just mastered greed.

Greed *hoards.*

Man *withholds.*

Satan *steals.*

The nature of God alone is the giving nature. When you give, you have just revealed the nature of God inside you.

The only pleasure God receives is through *acts of faith.* His only need is to be believed. His greatest need is to be believed. "God is not a man, that He should lie," (Numbers 23:19).

If an unbeliever runs to a pastor after church and says, "I want to give my heart to Christ, pastor." The pastor prays. Suppose the unbeliever then says, "Will you pray that God will give me peace and forgiveness for my confession?"

Imagine a pastor who would reply with indignation—"Of course not! That's greedy. You want something back for giving your heart to Christ?" You would be shocked if your pastor said this.

Your Father offers supply for Seed; forgiveness for confession; order for chaos.

When Jesus talked to the woman at the well of

Samaria, He promised her water that she would never thirst again. Was that *wrong* to offer her something if she pursued Him? Of course not. That was the purpose of the portrait of water—to motivate her and give her a reason for *obeying Him.*

One day, my dear friend Dwight Thompson, the powerful evangelist, told me a story about the papaya. Somebody counted 470 papaya seeds in a single papaya. Also, I've been told that one papaya seed would produce a plant containing 10 papayas. Now, if each of the 10 contained 470 seeds, there would be 4,700 papaya seeds in one plant.

Now, just suppose you replant those 4,700 seeds to create 4,700 more plants. Do you know how much 5,000 plants containing 5,000 seeds would be? *Twenty five million seeds...on the second planting alone.*

And we are having trouble really believing in the hundredfold return. Why?

Millions must *unlearn* the poisonous and traitorous teaching that it is wrong to expect anything in return.

6 Facts You Should Know About The Law of Expectation

1.   **Expectation Is The Powerful Current That Makes The Seed Work For You.** "But without faith it is impossible to please Him: for he that cometh to God must believe that He is, and that He is a rewarder of them that diligently seek Him," (Hebrews 11:6).

2.   **Expect Protection As He Promised.** "And I will rebuke the devourer for your sakes, and he shall

not destroy the fruits of your ground; neither shall your vine cast her fruit before the time in the field, saith the Lord of hosts," (Malachi 3:11).

3. Expect Favor From A Boaz Close To You. "Give, and it shall be given unto you; good measure, pressed down, and shaken together, and running over, shall men give into your bosom. For with the same measure that ye mete withal it shall be measured to you again," (Luke 6:38).

4. Expect Financial Ideas And Wisdom From God As A Harvest. "But thou shalt remember the Lord thy God: for it is He that giveth thee power to get wealth," (Deuteronomy 8:18).

5. Expect Your Enemies To Fragment And Be Confused And Flee Before You. "The Lord shall cause thine enemies that rise up against thee to be smitten before thy face: they shall come out against thee one way, and flee before thee seven ways," (Deuteronomy 28:7).

6. Expect God To Bless You For Every Act of Obedience. "And it shall come to pass, if thou shalt hearken diligently unto the voice of the Lord thy God, to observe and to do all His commandments which I command thee this day, that the Lord thy God will set thee on high above all nations of the earth: And all these blessings shall come on thee, and overtake thee, if thou shalt hearken unto the voice of the Lord thy God," (Deuteronomy 28:1-2).

A businessman approached me. "I don't really believe Jesus really meant what He said about the hundredfold. We've misunderstood that."

"So, you intend to teach Jesus how to talk when you get to Heaven?" I laughed.

If He will do it for a papaya...He will do it for you and me. We are His children, not merely fruit on a tree!

I believe one of the major reasons people do not experience a supernatural abundant Harvest in finances is because they really do not expect Jesus to do what He said He would do.

Low expectations affect God.

When you sow with *expectation,* your Seed will stand before God as a testimony of your faith and confidence.

- ▶ Sow *expecting* God to respond favorably to every act of confidence in Him.
- ▶ Sow from *every* paycheck.
- ▶ Sow *expectantly, generously and faithfully.*

When you start looking and expecting God to fulfill His promise, the Harvest you have needed for so long will come more quickly and bountifully than you have ever dreamed.

Millions are not experiencing increase because nobody has yet told them about the Principle of Seed-faith.

The unlearned are simply the untaught.

Teachers are necessary. You would not have the ability to even read this book, but a teacher entered your life. You sat at their feet. You learned the alphabet. Hour after hour you sat through boring, agitating and often frustrating moments. But, it opened the Golden Door to Life.

You can only know something you have heard. Something you have been taught. That is why God calls mentors, ministers of the gospel, and parents to impart knowledge. "And He gave some, apostles; some, prophets; and some, evangelists; and some, pastors and teachers; For the perfecting of the saints, for the work of the ministry, for the edifying of the body of Christ...That we henceforth be no more children, tossed to and fro, and carried about with every wind of doctrine," (Ephesians 4:11-12, 14).

Everyone understands sowing. Sowing is planting a Seed in soil for a desired Harvest and return.

Seed-faith is sowing a specific Seed in faith that it will grow a Harvest throughout your life. It is deciding what kind of Harvest you want to grow and sowing a Seed to make it happen.

Seed-faith is letting go of something you have been given to create something else you have been promised.

Seed-faith is using something you have to create something else you want. When You Let Go of What Is In Your Hand, God Will Let Go of What Is In His Hand.

Your *Seed* is what blesses somebody else.

Your *Harvest* is anything that blesses you.

So, Seed-faith is sowing something you possess in faith that God will honor it by bringing a Harvest you desire back to you.

Now, most people have never understood the wonderful, glorious part of this principle of sowing and reaping. In fact, it is usually a threat. You will hear a parent tell a rebellious teenager, "Some day, you're going to reap what you sow!" Now, they rarely say that to the teenager when he is obedient and doing something wonderful. They only emphasize that when they are focusing on something *wrong* that the teenager did!

Every minister has used Galatians 6:7 to motivate their congregation to have a healthy fear of God. "Be not deceived; God is not mocked: for whatsoever a man soweth, that shall he also reap." But, if you keep reading after that verse, it is a wonderful and powerful promise that concludes, "but he that soweth to the Spirit shall of the Spirit reap life everlasting. And let us not be weary in well doing: for in due season we shall reap, if we faint not," (Galatians 6:7-9).

The Apostle Paul continues emphasizing this incredible and miraculous Principle of Seed-faith. It is his personal encouragement in using this principle to help people *do something wonderful for others*. "As we have therefore opportunity, let us do good unto all men, especially unto them who are of the household of faith," (Galatians 6:10).

The Principle of sowing and reaping in Scripture is not a threat. It is a wonderful and glorious promise to believers that *patience in sowing Seed will produce a Harvest worthy of pursuit.*

The Principle: *You can decide any Harvest God wants you to reap and sow a special Seed, wrapped with your faith, for a desired result.*

This is Seed-faith.

God works this principle *continually.* He had a Son, Jesus. But, He wanted a family. So, He planted His best Seed on a place called Calvary to produce a glorious family, the body of Christ. Here we are!

Elijah, the remarkable prophet, understood this principle as much as any other person in Scripture. He looks in the face of an impoverished peasant woman about to eat her last meal. Her son was shriveled and withered, emaciated, laying in the bed. She is destitute. This is not simply a widow needing more money to make a car note, or pay for her house. Her last piece of bread is the only thing between her and starvation.

But, God had smiled on her. Oh, He did not bring her a bag of groceries! You see, even that bag of groceries had an end to it. Elijah did not hand her a $20 bill. That would merely delay starvation a few more hours.

God sent her a man who understood how to keep creating Harvest after Harvest after Harvest with a simple Seed. Oh, it is a marvelous day in your life when God sends someone who can see the future of your Seed! You have found favor with angels! You have found favor that will outlast your trial! You may be staring at your present with total discouragement, but that man of God has a *picture of your future*.

Elijah did not say, "I will tell the church about your problem and see if anyone can help you." He did not criticize her. He did not ask her if she had been tithing. He pointed to something *she already had* and told her how to use it as a *bridge out of trouble*.

▶ You see, your Seed is the only *exit* from your present.

▶ Your Seed is the only *door* into your future.

▶ Your Seed is the *bridge of blessing* into the world you have dreamed of your entire life.

Elijah did something glorious and wonderful. Something I wish every man of God would do when he stands behind his pulpit and talks to people about an offering for the work of God. He explained that what she already had in her hand *contained the solution to her life*.

Seed-faith is bringing people beyond the porch of their problem and bringing them into the House of Wisdom, and showing them that every solution to their life is right there in their own hand!

The unconverted can feel empty and hopeless. But, God teaches that the Seed for their salvation is already in their mouth. "The word is nigh thee, even in thy mouth, and in thy heart: that is, the word of faith, which we preach; That if thou shalt confess with thy mouth the Lord Jesus, and shalt believe in thine heart that God hath raised Him from the dead, thou shalt be saved. For with the heart man believeth unto right-eousness; and with the mouth confession is made unto salvation," (Romans 10:8-10).

Think about it! You may be backslidden, broken, tormented and burdened down. Your sins number into hundreds. Yet, right where you sit this very moment *you can plant a Seed.* What is the Seed? *Your confession of Christ.* In a single second, millions have moved from a life of emptiness and hopelessness into light and joy.

A single Seed of confession can bring a person out of trouble for the rest of their life. That is Seed-faith. The glorious principle of Seed-faith. Everybody believes in sowing. Few have embraced the Harvest.

5 Reasons Ministers Do Not Teach On Sowing And Reaping

1. Some Have Not Taught It Because They Fear Criticism. You see, when you begin to talk about money, you are focusing on the core of your life. Money is the god of this world. *Everything* revolves around it. Powerful ministries avoid this topic like the plague. Yet, in the privacy of their leadership sessions, they weep and intercede for God to provide more finances so they can reach this generation.

2.   Some, Refusing To Discuss The Principle of Sowing And Reaping Publicly, Approach The Wealthy In The Privacy of Their Homes. There, they request and ask for large donations for their ministry.   Through this means, they deflect any criticism that could come from public emphasis.

3.   Some Feel That It Is Unbalanced To Talk About Money In A Church Service. Yet, nobody considers a dentist unbalanced because he works only on teeth.   Nobody considers a lawyer unbalanced because he only discusses legal matters.

Few become angry at an evangelist for preaching salvation.   Few become furious with a pastor teaching on the principles of loving relationships.   Everyone gets excited when thousands receive their healing in a miracle service.

But, the moment money is discussed, *another spirit enters the arena.* The atmosphere *changes.* The climate is *different.*

4.   Some Do Not Teach On The Principles of Prosperity Because Their Own Supply Is Sufficient. Recently, I walked into a million dollar home.   It was the residence of a minister friend. He never preaches on financial prosperity.   Souls are his focus. He is brilliant at building homes for a profit. He has friends who build him a home. He moves in. Later, when he sells it, he makes a generous profit.   Over the years, he has made a tremendous amount of money. He has no financial problems whatsoever because of his gift of building.   He understands contracting, and everything that goes along with it.

Many do not have this knowledge and background. So, while he enjoys the beautiful luxury of his million dollar home, thousands sit under his ministry who can hardly make their car payment. Their homes are tiny, cramped and uncomfortable. You see, *supply is not his focus any more.* So, it has never dawned on him that others have a problem he does not have.

5. Some Do Not Teach About Sowing For A Harvest Because of The Anger, Retaliation And Fierce Attack That It Attracts To Their Ministry. Nobody who wants to be productive has time for battle. Several years ago a powerful minister ministered to millions on television. When the media began to set a trap and strategy to destroy him, it cost him millions in lawyer fees. His staff became so fragmented, their focus was broken. Instead of writing books that helped people, he had to meet with lawyers for hundreds of hours. His tax records were analyzed. They searched through garbage containers to find financial documents and letters from partners.

The ungodly will invest millions to shut the mouth of one man of God. So, many men of God will avoid this teaching so they can *retain their focus* on people instead of defending their ministry. It is costly. It is devastating, physically and spiritually.

Consequently, their people plunge into poverty and losses because *they remain untaught.*

Something intrigues me. When the discussion of money and giving to the work of God emerges, *the ungodly find a common ground with many religious leaders.* They join together—like Pontius Pilate with the Pharisees of his day for the common goal of crucifying Jesus of Nazareth.

Why is there anger over the message of sowing Seed to create a financial Harvest in your personal life?

Do these people despise giving? I don't think so. You see, our entire earth is a giving earth. Thousands give to the March of Dimes, Muscular Dystrophy, the Red Cross and the Salvation Army. Nobody is angry about your giving...to other people. The anger involves *giving to the work of God.*

Are they angry because teaching on prosperity is unnecessary and wasted time? Of course not. Most people do not have enough money to pay their present bills. Most do not even have a car that is paid for. Someone has said 60 percent of Americans would be bankrupt within 90 days if their job was stopped or terminated. No, the anger is not because everyone has too much money. Everyone is needy.

Is the anger directed toward all the ministers of the gospel for receiving offering? I do not believe so. I see many ministers on television who are not criticized when they simply announce that there is a need for an offering so they can build a cathedral. The greatest evangelist of our generation receives offerings in every crusade. He has never been criticized, because his offerings are very low key.

No, the anger is not over receiving offerings. That has gone on for hundreds of years. The anger is not over a church that needs help or widows who need assistance.

Do those who fight the Seed-faith message of prosperity despise money and hate the subject of money? Not at all. I watched a talk show host recently. He blasted his anger fiercely at ministers who taught about sowing to produce prosperity. Then he offered his own video at the end of his program for $40. So, he does not hate money. He wants more of it for himself. He is not anti-money. He certainly is not anti-making a profit, since the average video costs about $2.50.

Those who become infuriated over sowing toward prosperity are angry that a minister promises a hundredfold return from God for their Seed. They hate the teaching that you can "give something you have and get something back in return from God."

The battle is over Expectation of a Harvest.

Let's analyze this. Are they angry because they believe God *cannot* give a Harvest? Most people believe God can do anything.

Do these believe that God *should not* produce a Harvest from our Seed? I do not think so. Every television reporter searches for impoverished ghetto areas to stir up the consciousness of America toward the poor. Thousands even get angry at God for not doing something for them. Most every human believes God should prosper him.

Do they believe that God *will not* really prosper people who sow into His work?

Now, there is a lot of controversy over this.

Here is one of the greatest discoveries of my life. The anger over sowing Seed into the work of God to get a Harvest is because they believe it is wrong to expect something back from God.

The hated word is *expectation*.

"When I give to God, I expect nothing in return!" droned one religious leader recently. "I give because I love Him. I give because of obedience. It is greedy to expect something back in return." Yet, this same religious leader expects a paycheck every single week of his life—in return for his spiritual leadership.

It is only expecting *money* back from God that

produces the point of contention.

Is it wrong to give your heart to God and expect forgiveness, mercy and a home in Heaven. Oh, no! That is all right to expect an eternal home in return. Is it wrong to bring your sick body to God and expect Divine healing in return? Few disagree with that.

It is only money that bothers them. Money given to God and his work.

Why is it wrong to expect God to give a hundredfold return? This is not even logical. Think of the hundreds of doctrines taught in Scriptures. The doctrine of the blood, The Holy Spirit, angels and demons. Think of the horrifying consequences of sin, rebellion and witchcraft. If there should be rebellion to something taught in Scripture, why have we chosen to hate the Principle of Prosperity? It is against every part of our logic to hate something that brings blessing, provision and the ability to bless others.

This is a satanic thing. Oh, my friend, if you could see satan for what he really is, you would despise him with every ounce of your being. He is slimy, slick and deceptive. He truly is a serpent.

Why isn't there great anger and hatred over the preaching on hell? If I were going to refuse truth, it would be the belief in a hell. You see, it is not even natural to be anti-money.

Suppose you and I were shopping. As we walked through the mall, I saw a man huddled in the corner.

"Oh, there's a man who needs help. He looks hungry. His clothes look tattered. Let's do something good for him." You and I walk over to him.

"Sir, are you all right?"

"No," he mutters. "I have not eaten in 4 days. I

am out of work, and unemployed. I am homeless. Can
you help me in any way?"

You and I rejoice. Here is our chance to bless this
man. "Here, sir. Here is $20. Please buy yourself a
good meal at the cafeteria."

Now suppose this happened. He takes the $20 bill.
He tears it in pieces. He looks up at us angrily, "Why
are you trying to give me a $20 bill?"

You would call this insanity. I would agree. I
would say, "Here's a very sick man. He threw away
something that could change his pain into pleasure. I
handed him an answer, a solution, some money. He acts
like it is a trap, a trick, poison."

Yet, the great Provider of this universe hands us
the Principle of Prosperity that will rewrite our
financial future, and we erupt with anger at the
thought that we could sow a Seed and reap a Harvest!

This is insanity! It is not insanity of the mind, it
is insanity of the will, the *chosen* path of rebellion.

Are we against money? Of course not. When we
find a quarter on the pavement, we tell every friend on
the telephone that day. When we discover a $20 bill
forgotten in the pocket of our old clothes in the corner
of our closet, we shout! It brings fresh motivation into
us. Maybe it does not take a lot to excite us these
days—just the unexpected.

The entire warfare over the Seed-faith message
and the principles of prosperity is over this—
expectation of a financial Harvest back from God.

Now, here is the most incredible truth:

*Expectation Is The Only Pleasure Man Can
Generate In The Heart of God.*

You see, faith is confidence in God.

Expectation is the evidence of your faith.

God said that it is impossible to pleasure Him *unless you expect something from Him.* "But without faith it is impossible to please Him: for he that cometh to God must believe that He is, and that He is a rewarder of them that diligently seek Him," (Hebrews 11:6).

You cannot even be saved *unless you expect Him* to receive you.

You cannot be healed unless you *expect Him* to heal you.

You cannot be changed unless you *expect Him* to change you.

His Only Pleasure Is To Be Believed.

His Only Pain Is To Be Doubted.

I will say it again, the essence of the entire Bible is Numbers 23:19: "God is not a man, that He should lie; neither the son of man, that He should repent: hath He said, and shall He not do it? or hath He spoken, and shall He not make it good?"

God is not a man.

Man lies. God *does not.*

Think about this! God is not pleasured by streets of gold, clouds of angels. He is only happy when somebody is expecting Him to do what He said. What is *believing? Expecting God to do something He said.*

This huge controversy is not even about you or your home. Your poverty is not the goal of satan. You are not the real enemy to him.

God is the real enemy of satan.

Satan knows what pleasures God—for a human to trust Him, believe Him, depend on Him. Satan remembers the presence of God. He is a former employee.

He is an angel who refused to believe God and is tasting the eternal consequences.

The goal of satan is to rob God of every moment of pleasure received from humans.

How can he rob God? *When he stops your expectation of a miracle, he has paralyzed and stopped the only pleasure God experiences.* Every time you expect a miracle, you create a river of pleasure through the heart of God. Every time you doubt, you create waves of pain. God has feelings too.

That is what is behind the *anti-prosperity cult* on earth.

They are not anti-money.

They are not against you having money.

They are against you expecting any money from God.

Oh, my precious friend, listen to my heart today. Why would men waste time, precious expensive television time, smearing, sneering and destroying other men of God who are praying for people to get out of poverty? This world is impoverished. Somebody said that 40 percent of bankruptcies involve born-again Christians. This world is experiencing the financial crush every day. You would think that everyone would praise, admire and encourage any man of God who wanted to see you blessed, pay your bills and send your children through college. Why aren't we thanking God aloud and often for the wonderful teaching that our Jehovah is a miracle God of provision?

It is not the teaching that you can have money that is bothering them.

It is the teaching that *God will supply you a*

Harvest when you release your Seed to Him.

When you involve "the expectation of a return" with an offering, you arouse every devil in hell who despises their former boss who is pleasured by your expectation.

They hate the God you love.

They are obsessed with *depriving Him of every possible moment of pleasure* you are creating in the heart of God.

Your Father simply wants to *be believed.* That is all. He just wants to be believed. In fact, He promised that if you would just put Him above everything else in your life, He would keep providing anything you needed *for the rest of your life.* (See Matthew 6:33.) *He wants to be believed.* He invited you to prove His Word to you. (Read Malachi 3:9-11.)

Here is the argument of the anti-prosperity cult. "What about greed? That is materialism. When you offer some money back for giving to God, that is satanic. That is ungodly! That is poisonous and deceptive to offer something back when they give to God."

Then, why did God offer us something back in return for Seed if that is greed? Do you feel that it is greedy to work for a salary? You are getting something in return!

God anticipated greed. He knew our need and desire for increase could be deceptive, distorted and easily used to manipulate us. So, He built in a "corrective."

He put something in the system of increase that would completely paralyze any problem with greed— GIVING.

It is impossible for you to give to God and stay

greedy.

That is why He established the tithing system of returning 10 percent back to Him.

That is why He promised Peter a hundredfold return for giving up everything to follow Christ. (Read Mark 10:28-30.)

Every person who sows their Harvest has just conquered greed.

Greed *hoards.*

God *gives.*

It is impossible to give your way to greed.

Now, inside of each of us is an invisible command to become more, to multiply and increase. The *first commandment* ever given by God in the first book of Genesis, was to multiply and replenish and *become more.*

God is a God of increase. It is normal to become more, desire more and produce more. Remember the story regarding the man with one talent? He was punished eternally. Why? He did not do anything with his gifts and skills to increase his life. In fact, what he had was given to another person who had multiplied, used his gifts and become productive.

God is not cruel. He is not a liar and deceptive. If He gives you a desire for increase and prosperity, *He will place something inside you that can correct the problem it produces.* Giving.

All the preaching against greed and materialism is *only necessary for non-tithers and non-givers.*

Any discussion with the giver about being greedy is totally unnecessary. His Seed is proof that he has conquered it. His Seed is the corrective to potential greed.

What you can walk away from is something you have mastered. What you cannot walk away from is something that has mastered you.

Weeping will not correct greed.

Screaming will not correct it.

Confession will not stop greed.

Sowing is the only known cure for greed.

Obedience. Just returning the tithe. Just replanting the Seed He put in your hand.

The entire warfare and controversy over prosperity is to stop God from feelings of pleasure and feeling good about creating humans. You are not the target. This whole controversy does not revolve around you and your family. This whole controversy is between satan and God. You are only caught in the crossfire.

My Seed is the only proof I am expecting something in return. The only evidence that a farmer is looking for a Harvest is when you see him sowing his Seed. Your Seed is the proof you are expecting.

Your words are not the proof. You can talk about many things and still not really be expecting a Harvest.

Now, *expectation is only possible when a Seed has been planted.*

While you are withholding from God, it is impossible for your faith to work and expectation to occur. So, when God speaks to your heart to sow a Seed, you cannot even begin to expect a Harvest until you have obeyed His instruction. Your obedience in sowing immediately possesses you to be able *to expect.*

Now, your sowing does not create expectation. It makes it *possible* for you to expect.

You see, many people sow but they have not been taught the principle of Seed-faith—that you should expect something in return. So millions give to churches and never see a huge return on their Seed. They give to pay the bills of the church. They give because of guilt over withholding after all the blessings they have experienced. They give because a pastor meets with them privately and insists on them making "a donation to the cause." They give for many reasons.

Few sow their Seed to produce a Harvest.

Few sow with *expectation of a real return* from God.

How do you know that most do not expect a return? *They become angry over sowing.* If you believed something was coming back to you a hundred times—you would be more excited in that moment than any other time of your life.

Example: Have you ever received a sweep-stakes letter in the mail that you have "won a million dollars?" Of course, you have. Now, when you are young and in-experienced, you get very excited. You tear the envelope open. You can just imagine yourself with a yacht, a beautiful Rolls Royce and a vacation to Spain. What is happening? *Expectation excites you,* energizes you and creates a flurry of enthusiasm around you.

Expectation.

After you tear the envelope open, you suddenly realize there was part of the letter you could not see when it was closed. The part that says, "You *could* be one of those who win a million dollars." After you open the letter, you realize that they did not promise that you won it. But, you *may have been* one of the winners. The expectation wanes and dies.

And withers. You make a telephone call and realize that you were not really one of the winners. Expectations dies. Disappointment sets in.

Any disappointment you are experiencing today reveals your lack of expectation of a Harvest.

So, watch and sense the atmosphere that fills a church when an offering is being received. If there is expectation of a Harvest, *joy will fill that house.*

If expectation is present, joy is present.

Joy is the proof of expectation.

Depression and disappointment are evidences of fear present. The fear of loss. The fear of less.

Expectation is an impossibility until you sow a Seed.

You can have a need and *still not expect an answer.*

You can have a great dream and *still not expect it to come to pass.*

Expectation is produced by *obedience.*

Obedience is the proof of faith.

Faith is confidence in God.

Peter declared that he had given up everything to follow Christ. What was the reaction of Jesus? Well, He did not commend him for discipleship. He did not commend him for his willingness to suffer. He did not brag on him for being a martyr. Jesus looks at him and promises that he will get everything back that he gave up, *one hundred times over.* (See Mark 10:28-30.)

Jesus constantly promoted expectation.

When the woman at the well of Samaria listened to Him, He promised her water that she would never thirst again. When the weary came to Him, He said, "I will give you rest." When the sinful approached Him with humility and confession, He promised them that they were forgiven.

Jesus always responded to those with great

expectation. When the blind man cried out and was instructed to be silent by the crowds, Jesus reacted. Many were blind. One had great expectations of Jesus. Jesus healed him.

Impossible things happen to those who expect them to happen. "For verily I say unto you, That whosoever shall say unto this mountain, Be thou removed, and be thou cast into the sea; and shall not doubt in his heart, but shall believe that those things which he saith shall come to pass, he shall have whatsoever he saith," (Mark 11:23).

▶ *Anything good is going to find you.*
▶ Anything from God is going to *search you out.*
▶ Anything excellent is going to become *obvious* to you.

That is the principle of Seed-faith.

You have something given to you by God that has a future. When you discover your Seed and wrap your faith around it with great expectation...you will produce the financial Harvest you have desired for your lifetime.

Our Prayer Together...

"Father, teach us the Wonder of Expectation. Show us how it pleasures You to be believed.

Hasten the Harvest as we depend on Your incredible integrity. In Jesus' name. Amen."

✖ 30 ✖

Sow Instantly In Obedience To The Holy Spirit Without Rebellion Or Negotiation

━━━━━━━━━●<►━━━━━━━━━

The Holy Spirit Will Not Argue With You.

He is the Gift of the Father to those who obey Him. He will woo you. He will tug on your heart. He is gentle, kind and long-suffering.

But, He will not enter into a debate with you. He despises strife, confusion and struggle. "And the servant of the Lord must not strive; but be gentle unto all men," (2 Timothy 2:24).

He will move away from your attacks and quarrelsome spirit. "But foolish and unlearned questions avoid, knowing that they do gender strifes," (2 Timothy 2:23).

Do not argue with the *Source of your supply.* Stop looking for reasons to avoid sowing. Honor His integrity. He is not unfair. He is not unjust. When He whispers to your heart to take a step of faith, leap forward. *Run toward your Harvest.*

"Well, I don't want to simply plant out of an

emotional feeling!" one minister friend of mine explained.

"Everything you do is emotional," I replied. "When you drag a moment of faith through the sewage of logic, you destroy its impact and influence. Be swift to obey His voice."

I experienced an unusual miracle in my life when I was about 23 years old. I had been on the evangelistic field two or 3 years. My first year as an evangelist brought me $2,263 income. (One month my entire income was $35. Another month it was $90. I lived in a house that my father had purchased for $150. The entire house!)

Eventually, I had enough money saved to buy a suit and some clothes. It had taken a good while, but I finally saved up $200. I had two $100 bills inside my wallet. I was rather proud and thankful for it. I felt secure. I was anxious to get to a store to buy me some clothes.

A young evangelist friend of mine was preaching in a local church. So, I decided to hear him. While he was speaking, I felt the inner tug of The Holy Spirit to plant the $200 into his ministry. I explained to the Lord that my plans were to purchase clothes, so I could look good for His work. The longer he ministered, the more miserable I felt. A heaviness was in me. I thought of every reason to keep the $200. Inside, I began to *negotiate* with The Holy Spirit. I really did not have a desire to plant any Seed whatsoever. But I knew His voice.

Somewhere, during some service of a man of God The Holy Spirit is going to raise your level of desire to *please Him.* You may not have a lot of joy during the sowing. You may even experience inner conflict and mind confusion, *but something in you will become so strong and intense* that your desire to please Him will overwhelm your logic, your fears and your greed. It is that miracle moment when your desire to obey Him becomes so powerful that you *open the windows of Heaven* toward your life.

After the service, I went to my evangelist friend and handed him the $200. He was thrilled. I was rather saddened but tried to hide it. It was my clothes money.

Seven days later, I was laying in bed at midnight. The telephone rang.

"Brother Mike Murdock?"

"Yes?"

"You don't really know me. My husband and I were in your services a year ago here in Memphis. My son died 4 weeks ago, and God told my husband and I to start treating you like our boy. God told us to buy you some clothes. Are you coming through Memphis any time soon?" *What do you think!* I didn't care if I had to go through Australia and Russia to get to Memphis, I was going to arrive in Memphis...*very soon!*

When I got off the plane, they took me to the nicest men's store in Memphis, Tennessee. They bought me 4 suits, shirts and shoes. Six months later, they did it again. Six months later, they did it again. Six months later, they did it again. And again. Again. And again.

I went to hear a friend of mine in Houston at his church on a Sunday night. Halfway through his sermon, he stopped. He pointed back to me on the back row and said, "It is so good to have Mike Murdock here tonight. The Holy Spirit just spoke to me to stop the

service and receive him an offering to buy him clothes."
I was stunned.

On a Wednesday night, I drove across town to another church. I had never met this pastor before. Halfway through his Bible study, he looks back and notices me on the back seat.

"I see Mike Murdock here tonight. Brother, you and I have never met before, but I have seen you in various conferences. It is wonderful to have you. The Holy Spirit just spoke to my heart to stop the service and receive you an offering to buy you some clothes."

Months later, I was in Louisville, Kentucky, and my pastor friend says, "What are you doing tomorrow morning?"

"What do you want to do?" I replied.

"The Holy Spirit spoke to my heart *to buy you some clothes.*" he replied.

I am sitting next to a minister friend of mine in Illinois. He leans over to me and whispers in church, "When are you leaving tomorrow?"

"Why?" I asked.

"I felt the Lord wanted me to *buy you a Brioni suit tomorrow.*" (The next day he purchased it for me. Though he got it wholesale, the retail price on it was $3,220!)

One of my closest friends, Nancy Harmon, called me to her house. I walked in and there were clothes from one end of the room to the other. "The Lord told me to *buy you some clothes,*" she said.

You see, I had walked away from my clothes money. Now, God was supernaturally talking to people about replacing my clothes money by purchasing clothes for me.

What You Are Willing To Walk Away From Determines What God Will Bring To You.

Please, never argue with the Source of every miracle you are desiring. *When He talks to you about a Seed, He has a Harvest on His mind.*

You see, He knew *the future* He was planning. So, He gave me faith to *plant the Seed that would create my desired future.* He gave me the desire, the Seed and the soil where it would grow the quickest.

You can *grieve* The Holy Spirit through debating.

You can cause Him to *withdraw* from you when you negotiate and *move away from faith.*

Faith attracts Him. Faith excites Him. Expectation is His pleasure. *Do not rob Him of that moment of obedience.*

Delayed obedience can become disobedience.

Millions have lost a thousand Harvests because they became intellectual, negotiating and argumentative when The Holy Spirit began to whisper an instruction to their heart.

I was in Jacksonville, Florida, a few days ago. The secretary of the pastor came to me weeping. Her husband was by her side.

"Here is the best Seed God has told us to sow. Please take it." It was her wedding rings, the most precious treasure she had. (When you plant a Seed that you can feel, God will feel too. You must plant something significant to you before it becomes significant to God.)

That was Monday night.

Five days later, Friday night, she stood at a special School of The Holy Spirit with incredible joy on her countenance and gave her testimony. Somebody, who knew nothing of their sacrificial Seed of all of her rings, had decided to bless her; they became a Boaz to her. *They gave her a ring worth 100 times the cost of her own rings.*

"And Jesus answered and said, Verily I say unto you, There is no man that hath left house, or brethren, or sisters, or father, or mother, or wife, or children, or lands, for My sake, and the gospel's, But he shall receive an hundredfold now in this time, houses, and brethren, and sisters, and mothers, and children, and lands, with persecutions; and in the world to come eternal life," (Mark 10:29-30).

God is *not a man* that He should lie.

He wants to be *believed.*

▶ Nobody can *use your faith for you.*

▶ Nobody can *dream bigger for you.*

▶ Nobody can *plant the Seed for you.*

Nobody. Not your mother, nor father, nor boss, nor child.

Every man will give an account of himself to God.

Sometimes, I picture this scenario. Everybody is approaching the Throne of Accountability. Somebody wants answers to some questions. They want God to explain *why they were poor.* And He will ask the same question.

"Why were you poor when I promised you one hundredfold return for anything you would plant in My work? I told you if you would obey My principles, be diligent and expect Me to do what I promised, I would open the windows of Heaven and pour you out a blessing that you could not receive. I, too, want to know why you decided to disregard My instructions and remain without the Financial Harvest?"

That might be the *Weeping Night of Eternity* when everybody recognizes that the principles were accessible, available and usable—but ignored.

Now, you can begin your own journey to prosperity. Be willing to take it a step at a time. Do not rush it. Be careful to obey His voice. *Review* this book carefully. Bring it with you into *The Secret Place* of prayer. Talk to The Holy Spirit and ask Him *every single step* you should take at this time. Bring your stack of bills and credit cards and place them on top of this book. Anoint them, and *invite the supernatural intervention* of God to break the financial poverty and spirit of lack that has affected and influenced your life.

▶ Ask God to give you a hatred of poverty and a love and desire for supernatural provision.

▶ Discuss your dreams and financial goals in detail with Him.

▶ Believe that He will send a Boaz into your life to bless you in many ways.

When He talks to your heart about planting a Seed into His work, do not hesitate. Do not negotiate. And, do not manipulate. The Holy Spirit honors integrity where He finds it.

Confess any sin. Admit if you have withheld the tithes and the offerings He asked. Repent with humility, integrity and expectation of a change in your life.

You will see the changes come sooner than you dreamed.

Today is the poorest you will ever be the rest of your life.

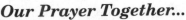

Our Prayer Together...

"Father, I've opened my heart, and sowed the revelation that changed my life forever. Now, use this Seed to grow an Uncommon Harvest. Oh, bless the obedient, the willing and the hungry. In Jesus' name. Amen."

RECOMMENDED INVESTMENTS:
The Covenant of Fifty-Eight Blessings (Book/B-47/82 pgs)
My Seed Testimony (Book/B-242/32 pgs)

≈ **31** ≈

The Greatest Success Secret God Has Ever Taught Me

━━━━━◆━━━━━

Some Years Ago Something Happened To Me That Literally Changed The Course of My Life.

It revolutionized my ministry.

It transformed me.

It made me a whole different person.

I was out in the garage that I had made into a make-shift office. I had been working for hours trying to catch up with some of my mail, filling orders, studying, writing and praying. I had been fasting 5 days.

On the fifth day at 2:30 a.m., God spoke to my heart...not aloud, but into my very spirit and innermost being. It was a simple sentence. But, it struck me with the force of a sledge-hammer blow. It echoed and resounded inside my head and engraved itself on the very walls of my heart.

What was the message?

"What You Make Happen For Others, I Will Make Happen For You."

I realized God was speaking to me. He burned this truth deep within my consciousness. Over and over those words came to me, and more and more I began to think this was the "Golden Thread" in the Garment of Life.

If I make good things happen for others, God will make good things happen for me. If I cause bad things to happen to others, bad things will happen to me. It works both ways. And it works always...*without fail.*

Now, all of my life I had been taught that where I sowed, there would I reap. But, the real truth is...*what* I sow I will reap, not *where* I sow. I may not reap from the same place I sow. God may have me sow Seeds in one person's field, and when Harvest time comes, I may reap *from* the field of *someone else.* This is because the Source of my Harvesting is not the caretaker of the field—but God, *who owns all.*

What I make happen for others, God will make happen for me. That is the *secret.* That is the understanding that becomes your *Key to Success.* Do not look for your Harvest *where* you have sowed. Look for your Harvest *because* you have sowed.

Create success situations for others around you. Do not be surprised or alarmed if they fail to return the favor. You sow into the lives of others, but your *expectation of return is from God,* your Heavenly Father...your Source.

So, the basic law is very simple.

If you want to be a success...if you want to be fulfilled...concentrate on the success and fulfillment of others. Get your mind off yourself. Quit talking about your needs and your desires. Think of ways to create success for *the people around you.* Help *them* reach their goals. Help them become fulfilled and happy.

It guarantees your own success.

What happens when you do this? *When you make others successful, you create a "zone" of success.* As you make the people around you successful, you are caught up in the middle of that success zone. And *what you have made happen for others, God will make happen for you.*

As I said earlier, this principle works both ways...for good or *bad.* Remember the story of Jacob in the Bible? He deceived his dying father to receive for himself the blessing that should have been his brother's. But only a few years later, Jacob was deceived by his uncle, Laban. After working 7 years to gain the hand of the fair Rachel in marriage, Jacob was given the older sister, Leah. He had to work 7 more years for the girl he really loved.

What he made happen for someone else... deception...happened to him.

It also happens for *good.* Read 1 Kings 17:8-16, and you will find a fascinating success story. When a poor widow risked personal starvation in order to "create a success situation" for the prophet Elijah, God made that same miracle provision happen to her. *What she made happen for Elijah, God made happen for her!*

Though Job had experienced tremendous tragedies in his personal life, *he got his mind off his own troubles and began to pray for his friends instead.* Then his own miracle happened...the Lord turned his captivity! "And the Lord turned the captivity of Job, when he prayed for his friends: also the Lord gave Job twice as much as he had before," (Job 42:10).

Some time after God dealt with me so strongly on this subject, I was ministering in New Orleans, Louisiana. I urged the congregation to concentrate their efforts on making others successful, and that God would make them successful. One young man really took my challenge to heart. He decided to put the principle to work with his boss.

He went to his employer and said, "I want to be your 'Success-Maker.' I want to make you more successful than you have ever been—the best boss you have ever been. I want you to make more money than you have ever made before. Just tell me what I can do to help you be more successful. Give me some of *your most difficult tasks* to do so you will be free to become more productive."

The young man's boss was completely shocked. He said, "No one has ever said that to me before. Tell me, why do you want to make me successful? What do *you* want out of it?"

The boy said, "I believe if I make you successful, then God will make me successful. If I help you to make more money for this business, then you will be able to pay me more. You'll be more successful, and so will I. I have wanted to make $6 an hour instead of $5. If I help you reach your goal, you will probably be able to help me achieve mine."

The boss said, "You will get your raise today. Anyone who cares about my success that much is surely worth $6 an hour!"

I believe with all my heart that this is one of the laws of God. *What You Make Happen For Others, God Will Make Happen For You.* Let this principle become part of the fabric of your Wisdom, and it will become a Golden Key in your hand to open every Room of Success you come to.

So start now. *Concentrate on the success of those around you.* How can you make your wife, your husband, your children more successful? How can you help your business or employer succeed in a greater way? What can you do to bless your church? Look for new ways to make everybody *around you* more successful. When you find such an opportunity, be quick to carry it out.

As you make them successful, God will bless you with success. "Knowing that whatsoever good thing any man doeth, the same shall he receive of the Lord," (Ephesians 6:8).

Jesus was the world's greatest Success-Maker. He *came* to make men successful. He is the original Success-Maker. He came to upgrade men and women, and yes, even teenagers and children.

God made you in His image. You are important and valuable to Him. You are an extension of His life and personality. "For whom He did foreknow, He also did predestinate to be conformed to the image of His Son, that He might be the firstborn among many brethren. Moreover whom He did predestinate, them He also called: and whom He called, them He also justified: and whom He justified, them He also glorified. What shall we then say to these things? If God be for us, who can be against us? He that spared not His own Son, but delivered Him up for us all, how shall He not with Him also freely give us all things? Who shall lay any thing to the charge of God's elect? It is God that justifieth," (Romans 8:29-33).

You can be like Him. That is the way He meant for you to be. "Beloved, now are we the sons of God, and it doth not yet appear what we shall be: but we know that, when He shall appear, we shall be like Him; for we shall see Him as He is. And every man that hath this hope in Him purifieth himself, even as He is pure," (1 John 3:2-3).

"For ye are all the children of God by faith in Christ Jesus. For as many of you as have been baptized into Christ have put on Christ. There is neither Jew nor Greek, there is neither bond nor free, there is neither male nor female: for ye are all one in Christ Jesus. And if ye be Christ's, then are ye Abraham's Seed, and heirs according to the promise," (Galatians 3:26-29).

But what is God like? Most of us have a very muddled vague, hazy opinion of who God is. I heard about a mother who came upon her little boy busily drawing and coloring at his table. "What are you drawing, son?" she asked.

"A picture of God," he said.

"But, Billy, nobody knows what God looks like," she told him.

The youngster thought about it a moment, then announced matter-of-factly, *"They will when I get through."*

Oh, how I wish every minister of the gospel succeeded with that goal! It's so hard to explain beauty in a world that is often ugly and destructive. *God is a good God.*

Jesus came to show us what God is like. "...he that hath seen me hath seen the Father," (John 14:9). *His whole purpose was to make you successful and show you what you are capable of becoming...of doing...of possessing.* "No man hath seen God at any time; the only begotten Son, which is in the bosom of the Father, He hath declared Him," (John 1:18).

Take a look at the life of Jesus. He proved His power as a *Success-Maker.* He devoted His entire earthly ministry and life to helping people become more than they were, and to have more than they *had*. "The thief cometh not, but for to steal, and to kill, and to destroy: I am come that they might have life, and that they might have it more abundantly. I am the good shepherd: the good shepherd giveth His life for the sheep," (John 10:10-11).

"How God anointed Jesus of Nazareth with the Holy Ghost and with power: Who went about doing good, and healing all that were oppressed of the devil; for God was with Him," (Acts 10:38).

When Jesus saw people who were lonely, He spent time with them and had fellowship with them. "And when Jesus came to the place, He looked up, and saw him, and said unto him, Zacchaeus, make haste, and come down; for to day I must abide at thy house. And he made haste, and came down, and received him joyfully," (Luke 19:5-6).

When Jesus saw people who were sick, He healed them. "And Jesus went about all the cities and villages, teaching in their synagogues, and preaching the gospel of the kingdom, and healing every sickness and every disease among the people," (Matthew 9:35).

When Jesus saw people who were hungry and faint, He fed them. "Then Jesus called His disciples unto Him, and said, I have compassion on the multitude, because they continue with Me now three days, and have nothing to eat: and I will not send them away fasting, lest they faint in the way," (Matthew 15:32).

When Jesus saw people who were timid or bound by mediocrity, He challenged them to stand up, step out, launch out. "And they came to Him, and awoke Him, saying, Master, Master, we perish. Then He arose, and rebuked the wind and the raging of the water: and they ceased, and there was a calm. And He said unto them, Where is your faith?" (Luke 8:24-25).

Jesus understood people, because He saw them through the eyes of His Father. "The Spirit of the Lord is upon Me, because He hath anointed Me to preach the gospel to the poor; He hath sent Me to heal the broken-hearted, to preach deliverance to the captives, and recovering of sight to the blind, to set at liberty them that are bruised, To preach the acceptable year of the Lord," (Luke 4:18-20). That is why He could make them successful, *for Wisdom is God's Golden Key to Success.*

What You Make Happen For Others, God Will Make Happen For You.

When Jesus saw people who were eager to know more, He taught them. "And seeing the multitudes, He went up into a mountain: and when He was set, His disciples came unto Him: And He opened His mouth, and taught them," (Matthew 5:1-2).

Jesus understood the needs of the people and met those needs in such a way as to make them successful. The key to their success was Wisdom—*developing a new picture of themselves in God's image.*

The picture you develop for yourself is critical to your success or failure. God wants you to see yourself as His highest creation.

- ▶ He is pouring His *mind* into you.
- ▶ He is pouring His *power* into you.
- ▶ He is pouring His *sensitivity* into you.
- ▶ He is pouring His *Wisdom* into your life.

"But if our gospel be hid, it is hid to them that are lost: In whom the god of this world hath blinded the minds of them which believe not, lest the light of the glorious gospel of Christ, Who is the image of God, should shine unto them," (2 Corinthians 4:3-4).

"Now the Lord is that Spirit: and where the Spirit of the Lord is, there is liberty. But we all, with open face beholding as in a glass the glory of the Lord, are changed into the same image from glory to glory, even as by the Spirit of the Lord," (2 Corinthians 3:17-18).

See yourself as a problem-solver for others...a success-maker for God.

Remember—*What You Make Happen For Others, God Will Make Happen For You.*

The Greatest Success Secret God Ever Taught Me

Here you have it! After 62 years of walking with God, and studying the Principles of Success, I am convinced the 3 most important things in your life are The Holy Spirit, The Assignment and The Seed. These chapters have been excerpts from the following books: 1) *The Holy Spirit Handbook,* 2) *The Assignment* (Volumes 1, 2 and 3) and *31 Reasons People Do Not Receive Their Financial Harvest.* For more complete information, I encourage you to order the complete volumes.

Yours For His Wisdom,

Mike Murdock

DECISION

Will You Accept Jesus As Your Personal Savior Today?

The Bible says, "That if thou shalt confess with thy mouth the Lord Jesus, and shalt believe in thine heart that God hath raised Him from the dead, thou shalt be saved," (Romans 10:9).

Pray this prayer from your heart today!

"Dear Jesus, I believe that You died for me and rose again on the third day. I confess I am a sinner...I need Your love and forgiveness...Come into my heart. Forgive my sins. I receive Your eternal life. Confirm Your love by giving me peace, joy and supernatural love for others. Amen."

DR. MIKE MURDOCK

is in tremendous demand as one of the most dynamic speakers in America today.

More than 23,000 audiences in over 133 countries have attended his Schools of Wisdom and conferences. Hundreds of invitations come to him from churches, colleges and business corporations. He is a noted author of over 900 books, including the best sellers, *The Leadership Secrets of Jesus* and *Secrets of the Richest Man Who Ever Lived.* Thousands view his weekly television program, *Wisdom Keys with Mike Murdock.* Many attend his Schools of Wisdom that he hosts in many cities of America.

Clip and Mail

☐ Yes, Mike, I made a decision to accept Christ as my personal Savior today. Please send me my free gift of your book, *31 Keys to a New Beginning* to help me with my new life in Christ.

NAME _____ BIRTHDAY _____

ADDRESS _____

CITY _____ STATE ___ ZIP ___

PHONE _____ E-MAIL _____ DFC

Mail to: **The Wisdom Center** · 4051 Denton Hwy. · Ft. Worth, TX 76117
1-817-759-BOOK · 1-817-759-2665 · 1-817-759-0300
MikeMurdockBooks.com

238

7 DECISIONS THAT DETERMINE YOUR PERSONAL SUCCESS

All of Your Success Comes Through Wisdom.

Your Wisdom determines the quality of your decisions. Everything you want comes through Wisdom and your decisions. The Bible is a book about decisions. There are 7 decisions that you will make that will decide Your Personal Success..!

1. Your Decision To Embrace The Word of God As Infallible And Unfailing.

"Keep therefore and do them; for this is your Wisdom and your understanding in the sight of the nations, which shall hear all these statutes, and say, Surely this great nation is a wise and understanding people," (Deuteronomy 4:6). "And thou shalt teach them diligently unto thy children, and shalt talk of them when thou sittest in thine house, and when thou walkest by the way, and when thou liest down, and when thou risest up," (Deuteronomy 6:7). "Thy word have I hid in mine heart, that I might not sin against Thee," (Psalm 119:11). "Remember the word unto Thy servant, upon which Thou hast caused me to hope," (Psalm 119:49). "O how love I Thy law! it is my meditation all the day," (Psalm 119:97). "Thy word is a lamp unto my feet, and a light unto my path,"(Psalm 119:105). "Thy testimonies have I taken as an heritage for ever: for they are the rejoicing of my heart," (Psalm 119:111). "Thy word is true from the beginning: and every one of Thy righteous judgments endureth for ever," (Psalm 119:160). "Great peace have they which love Thy law: and nothing shall offend them," (Psalm 119:165).

2. Your Decision To Become A Lifetime Learner.

"Learn to do well; seek judgment, relieve the oppressed, judge the fatherless, plead for the widow," (Isaiah 1:17). "Study to shew thyself approved unto God, a workman that needeth not to be ashamed, rightly dividing the word of truth," (2 Timothy 2:15). "But grow in grace, and in the knowledge of our Lord and Saviour Jesus Christ. To Him be glory both now and for ever. Amen," (2 Peter 3:18).

3. Your Decision To Show Honor To The Scriptural Chain of Authority.

"Children, obey your parents in the Lord: for this is right," (Ephesians 6:1). "Submit yourselves to every ordinance of man for the Lord's sake: whether it be to the king, as supreme. For so is the will of God, that with well doing ye may put to silence the ignorance of foolish men," (1 Peter 2:13,

15). "Likewise, ye younger, submit yourselves unto the elder. Yea, all of you be subject one to another, and be clothed with humility: for God resisteth the proud, and giveth grace to the humble," (1 Peter 5:5).

4. Your Decision To Excel In Solving Problems For Someone Who Is Trusting You.
"A good name is rather to be chosen than great riches, and loving favour rather than silver and gold. Seest thou a man diligent in his business? he shall stand before kings; he shall not stand before mean men," (Proverbs 22:1, 29). "Then this Daniel was preferred above the presidents and princes, because an excellent spirit was in him; and the king thought to set him over the whole realm," (Daniel 6:3).

5. Your Decision To Identify The Divine Role of Every Relationship.
"For as the body is one, and hath many members, and all the members of that one body, being many, are one body: so also is Christ," (1 Corinthians 12:12). "That there should be no schism in the body; but that the members should have the same care one for another. And whether one member suffer, all the members suffer with it; or one member be honoured, all the members rejoice with it. Now ye are the body of Christ, and members in particular," (1 Corinthians 12:25-27). "For we are members of His body, of His flesh, and of His bones," (Ephesians 5:30).

6. Your Decision To Pursue Mentorship From Uncommon Financial Achievers.
"Where no counsel is, the people fall: but in the multitude of counsellors there is safety," (Proverbs 11:14). "And how I kept back nothing that was profitable unto you, but have shewed you, and have taught you publickly, and from house to house," (Acts 20:20).

7. Your Decision To Make The Holy Spirit Your Lifetime Counselor.
"In all thy ways acknowledge Him, and He shall direct thy paths," (Proverbs 3:6). "And thine ears shall hear a word behind thee, saying, This is the way, walk ye in it, when ye turn to the right hand, and when ye turn to the left," (Isaiah 30:21). "Howbeit when He, the Spirit of truth, is come, He will guide you into all truth: for He shall not speak of Himself; but whatsoever He shall hear, that shall He speak: and He will shew you things to come," (John 16:13).

CD/SOWL-173